MELTING
ARCTIC
ICE

By Carol Hand

ECOLOGICAL **DISASTERS**

Content Consultant

Edward Blanchard-Wrigglesworth
Research Assistant Professor
Department of Atmospheric Sciences
University of Washington

Essential Library

An Imprint of Abdo Publishing | abdopublishing.com

abdopublishing.com

Published by Abdo Publishing, a division of ABDO, PO Box 398166, Minneapolis, Minnesota 55439. Copyright © 2018 by Abdo Consulting Group, Inc. International copyrights reserved in all countries. No part of this book may be reproduced in any form without written permission from the publisher. Essential Library™ is a trademark and logo of Abdo Publishing.

Printed in the United States of America, North Mankato, Minnesota
042017
092017

Cover Photos: Sepp Friedhuber/iStockphoto, cover
Interior Photos: Sam Soja/The Canadian Press/AP Images, 4–5; Robert Simmon/NASA, 7 (top), 7 (bottom); Christopher Zappa, 9; Saul Loeb/AFP/Getty Images, 10; NASA/Chris Larsen/University of Alaska-Fairbanks, 11; Bernhard Edmaier/Science Source, 13; Nesrin Ozdemir/Shutterstock Images, 14–15; Peter Hermes Furian/Shutterstock Images, 16 (foreground); iStockphoto, 16 (background), 19, 31, 39, 40–41, 96, 98 (bottom left); Tatu Lajunen/Shutterstock Images, 17; Andreea Dragomir/Shutterstock Images, 21; Shutterstock Images, 22, 25, 80, 93, 98 (top), 99 (middle); Red Line Editorial, 23, 35, 44; Armin Rose/Shutterstock Images, 24; Dr. Juerg Alean/Science Source, 26, 98 (bottom right); Louise Murray/Science Source, 27, 51, 55; Bernhard Staehli/iStockphoto, 28; NOAA, 32; Bryan and Cherry Alexander/Science Source, 36–37; Steve Allen/Shutterstock Images, 42; Rintaro Sawano/Kyodo/AP Images, 45; Terri Butler Photography/Shutterstock Images, 46–47; BP/National Remote Sensing Centre Ltd/Science Source, 48; Science Source, 49, 83; Michael Szoenyi/Science Source, 50; Sepp Friedhuber/iStockphoto, 52–53; Dennis Fast/VWPics/Newscom, 58–59; Paul Loewen/iStockphoto, 60; Ted Kerasote/Science Source, 62–63; Simon Fraser/Science Source, 65, 99 (bottom); Eric Chretien/Gamma-Rapho/Getty Images, 66–67; Tannis Toohey/Toronto Star/Getty Images, 68–69, 99 (top); Robert Szymanski/Shutterstock Images, 71; John Gaps III/AP Images, 73; Ryerson Clark/iStockphoto, 75; Ricardo Bacchini/Shutterstock Images, 76–77; Mohammed Seeneen/AP Images, 81; Sander Meertin's Photography/Shutterstock Images, 85; Nicolas Primola/Shutterstock Images, 87; Spencer Platt/Getty Images News/Getty Images, 88–89; Kathy Willens/AP Images, 91; Joshua Stevens/Suomi National Polar-orbiting Partnership/National Snow and Ice Data Center/NASA, 97

Editor: Arnold Ringstad
Series Designer: Laura Polzin

Publisher's Cataloging-in-Publication Data

Names: Hand, Carol, author.
Title: Melting Arctic ice / by Carol Hand.
Description: Minneapolis, MN : Abdo Publishing, 2018. | Series: Ecological
   disasters | Includes bibliographical references and index.
Identifiers: LCCN 2016962236 | ISBN 9781532110252 (lib. bdg.) |
   ISBN 9781680788105 (ebook)
Subjects: LCSH: Climatic changes--Arctic regions--Juvenile literature. | Global
   warming--Juvenile literature. | Environmental degradation--Juvenile literature.
   | Ecological disturbances--Juvenile literature.
Classification: DDC 363.738--dc23
LC record available at http://lccn.loc.gov/2016962236

CONTENTS

Chapter
ONE

HOW DO WE KNOW IT'S MELTING?

On July 10, 1959, geologist Paul T. Walker and his colleague Albert Crary were exploring a glacier on Ward Hunt Island off the coast of Ellesmere Island in far northern Canada. That day, Walker built a small rock cairn and wrote a letter, which he enclosed in a bottle and buried under the cairn. In the letter, he explained that he had placed the cairn exactly 168.3 feet (51.3 m) from the edge of the glacier.[1] He asked whoever found his letter to measure the distance to the edge of the glacier again, and send the result to him at Ohio State University. In 2013, biologist Dr. Warwick Vincent and his colleague Denis Sarrazin discovered the bottle and letter. Following Walker's wish, they measured the distance to the glacier. They discovered it was now 401 feet (122 m) away.[2] In the 54 years since Walker first measured it, the glacier had retreated 233 feet (71 m). It was shrinking.

Walker did not live long enough to receive a response from Vincent. He died the same year he wrote the letter. He was only in his twenties. But Vincent remarked on Walker's brilliance in leaving this message for the future. In the 1950s, he says, "It was unthinkable that this would melt."[3] Walker was one of the first scientists to realize that the climate was warming, ice was melting, and future glaciers might look very different. His data point—a comparison of glacier change over time—is valuable, Vincent said. It is very old, very rare, and from an isolated location. Vincent and Sarrazin decided to carry on the tradition. They photographed Walker's letter, replaced it, and added a letter of their own. They asked the next finder to measure the distance to the glacier again and report back to them.

MEASURING ICE CHANGES

Finding Walker's decades-old letter was lucky, but scientists do not rely only on luck to learn about ice melt and glacier retreat. So, how do they know glaciers and ice sheets are retreating? How do they know sea ice is melting? How do they know how fast it is happening? One way is by using satellite imaging. Satellites in orbit around Earth monitor

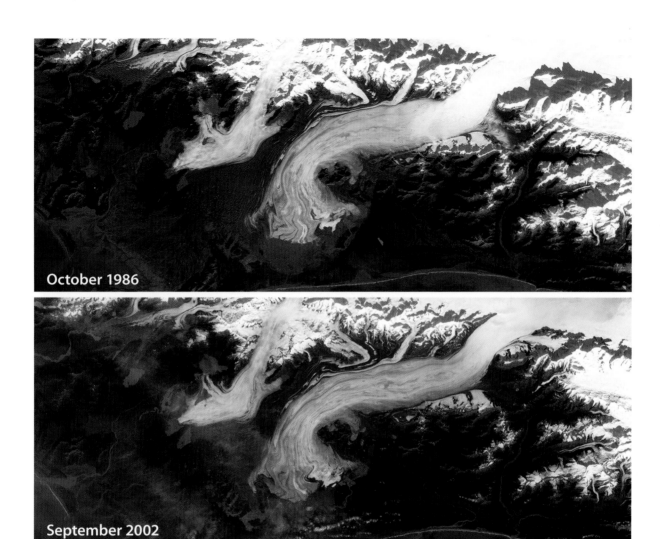

Satellite photos taken decades apart show changes in Alaska's Bering Glacier.

glaciers, ice sheets, and icebergs. When scientists compare images based on data taken at different times, they can observe changes in the extent of ice.

Other scientists study ice cores to understand the history of climate. They drill cores deep into ice sheets or glaciers and analyze gases trapped in bubbles within the ice. These gases provide glimpses of the composition of past atmospheres. They allow scientists to determine atmospheric temperature at those times. Scientists have used ice cores to build a picture of Earth's climate for the past 800,000 years. An understanding of past climates can help predict future climates, including rates of ice melt.

Scientists also make on-the-spot measurements of physical characteristics, including temperature, rates of glacier retreat, and rates of sea ice melt. Their tools range from sticks jammed in the ice to measure height to the latest scientific instruments. To measure changes in land ice, they travel over ice sheets, often in bitter cold and high winds. To measure sea ice, they conduct cruises on research vessels, dodging ice floes. One reason for on-the-spot investigations is simply that they bring home the reality of climate change and ice melt much more clearly than photographs or pages of numbers. Also, those firsthand observations and measurements can validate the data from satellite images.

SATELLITES PHOTOGRAPH ICE MELT

Surface ice on Greenland's ice sheet is the top of the ice only. The ice sheet is only a few meters thick at its edges, but toward the center it can be 10,500 feet (3,200 m, or almost 2 miles) thick.[4] On average, melt occurs over approximately one-half of the ice sheet's surface during the summer. But in 2012, melt occurred over nearly all of the surface. The melt progressed from approximately 40 percent on July 8 to 97 percent by July 12.[5] Surface meltwater quickly refreezes over most of the ice sheet. But near the coast, much of it drains into the ocean. The 2012 change was documented by three satellites, measuring different ice properties and passing over Greenland at different times. Lora Koenig, a glaciologist who helped analyze the data, says such extreme melts happen approximately every 150 years. The last one was in 1889. But if they continue to happen, as scientists expect, "it will be worrisome," Koenig says.[6]

MELTING SEA ICE

Scientists at the National Snow and Ice Data Center in Boulder, Colorado, have been collecting precise measurements of the extent of melting Arctic sea ice since 1978. Nearly 40 years of data show a clear, rapid melting trend. Ice amounts are always at their minimum during the month of September, at the end of summer melting. Since measurements began, total September ice coverage has decreased rapidly. In the 1980s, the Arctic contained approximately 773,200 square miles (2 million sq km) of old ice, or ice that is at least five years old. By 2010, there were only 22,000 square miles (57,000 sq km) of old ice—a decrease of more than 97 percent.[7]

Researchers are trying to figure out why Arctic ice is melting so rapidly. A 2015 international research expedition led by Harald Steen of the Norwegian Polar Institute surveyed a region around the North Pole on the RV (Research Vessel) *Lance*. The group spent an entire season on the ship, from January through the early summer ice breakup. They seldom used engines, instead drifting through ice floes, and worked through six weeks of the 24-hour darkness of polar winter. They explored nearby ice floes on foot, skis, and snowmobiles

DRONES MEASURE SEA ICE

Christopher Zappa uses unmanned airborne vehicles, or drones, to study Arctic ice melt. Drones get closer to the action than satellites and allow him to study much wider areas than when working from a research ship. "With drones," he says, "we can study melting and other processes as they're happening, on a very fine scale."[8] Zappa is an oceanographer at Columbia University's Lamont-Doherty Earth Observatory. He and his colleagues launch drones from the Svalbard Archipelago, a group of islands between Norway and the North Pole. Each eight-foot (2.4 m) drone carries up to 10 pounds (4.5 kg) of scientific instruments. They travel halfway to Greenland and back on each four-hour trip, skimming the water surface to make close-up observations. Different instrument packages measure variations in water and ice temperature, the structure of disintegrating ice, and ocean salinity, or saltiness.

RV *Lance* is one of many research ships that scientists use to study the extreme Arctic region.

and lowered buoys from the ship to measure water characteristics. They braved harsh winds and temperatures as low as -40 degrees Fahrenheit (-40°C) to study the formation and breakup of younger, thinner sea ice. They also had some confrontations with polar bears and had to be towed by the Norwegian Coast Guard after getting stuck in the ice. Yet such research voyages are essential to understanding how and why

> **"All the climatic processes seem to be pushing rapidly toward a seasonally ice-free Arctic Ocean."[9]**
>
> —*Dr. Julienne Stroeve, National Snow and Ice Data Center*

ice is melting now. They are also essential to understanding the future of Arctic ice.

CALVING GLACIERS

It is difficult to catch the process of calving as it happens. But sometimes good data—and a good movie—result from a combination of luck, preparedness, and perseverance. Just ask the film crew of the movie *Chasing Ice*, which centers on nature photographer James Balog. Balog's goal was to document the melting of Arctic ice due to climate change. He began his crusade to document climate change in 2005, when *National Geographic* sent him on assignment to the Arctic. Balog was originally a climate-change skeptic. He thought statements about climate change were based only on computer models, with no concrete measurements involved. But that first Arctic trip convinced him of the reality of climate change. He created the Extreme Ice Survey, an expedition that would keep him and a small group of intrepid explorers visiting the Arctic for years. They assembled a series of time-lapse cameras in the savage Arctic environment and kept them running. They captured years of ice footage and compressed it into seconds, documenting the movement and rapid disappearance of Arctic ice.

OPERATION ICEBRIDGE

The National Aeronautics and Space Administration (NASA) project Operation IceBridge has made airborne surveys of Arctic and Antarctic ice since 2009. IceBridge gives scientists a multiyear, three-dimensional view of ice sheets, ice shelves, and sea ice. It uses many instruments to show the rapid changes in polar ice. Arctic flights have gathered data on changing elevations and the internal structure of the Greenland ice sheet. They found a 460-mile (740 km) canyon beneath a mile (1.6 km) of ice, and a vast area of liquid water under the snow in southern Greenland.[10] IceBridge data helps scientists better predict the summer melt season and better understand yearly variations in ice thickness.

THE CALVING OF JAKOBSHAVN

The glacier calving in *Chasing Ice* was just one example of a continuing process. Huge chunks of ice are breaking off Greenland's glaciers with increasing regularity. Another massive event occurred in August 2015 and is called by scientists "one of the most significant calving events on record."[13] In this event, a chunk of ice measuring 4.2 cubic miles (17.5 cu km) broke off Greenland's Jakobshavn Glacier, the world's fastest-moving glacier. No one witnessed the event firsthand, but it was documented by radar images from the European Space Agency's (ESA) Sentinel-1A and Sentinel-2A weather satellites. The images showed the presence of the chunk of ice on August 14 and its absence on August 16. Jakobshavn Glacier is one of several glaciers along the Ilulissat fjord. Every year it generates 10 percent of all Greenland calf ice—more than any other glacier outside Antarctica.[14]

In 2012, Balog's crew waited weeks to catch the calving of Greenland's Jakobshavn Glacier. The crew had a front-row seat as a massive section of glacial ice—in this case, a volume of 1.8 cubic miles (7.4 cu km)—crashed into the surrounding ocean.[11] The result was the largest calving event ever filmed. With four separate time-lapse cameras set up and rolling, crew members Adam LeWinter and Jeff Orlowski watched, amazed, as a vast piece of the ice cliff began to break off. It took 75 minutes for all of the ice to break off and fall. LeWinter said, "The only way that you can really try to put it into scale with human reference is if you imagine Manhattan. . . . And all of a sudden, all of those buildings just start to rumble and quake, and peel off and fall over—fall over and roll around. This whole massive city just breaking apart in front of your eyes."[12]

The Jakobshavn Glacier retreated eight miles (12.9 km) during the entire 1900s. In the single decade from 2000 to 2010, it retreated nine miles (14.5 km). This provides one piece of evidence of the incredible rate of global warming. Altogether, evidence from around the world has scientists very worried. They are monitoring the calving of glaciers, and the rapid melting of sea ice. These measurements help them gauge the rate of global climate change. The rapid Arctic

The calving of a glacier can be an ear-splitting, ground-shaking event.

melting they are documenting will have implications not only in the Arctic, but also around the world. It will affect world ocean currents and climate. It will raise sea levels, changing the world's islands and coasts. It will affect every person on Earth.

"Ice is the canary in the global coal mine. It's the place where we can see and touch and hear and feel climate change in action."[15]

—James Balog, founder of Extreme Ice Survey

TWO

DEFINING ARCTIC ICE

The Arctic is the area around the North Pole. It consists of the Arctic Ocean, surrounded by the northern edges of North America, Europe, and Asia. Much of the region is covered by snow and ice. The southernmost boundary of the Arctic consists of boreal forests made up of evergreen trees such as spruce and fir. Between the icy ocean and the boreal forests is the tundra, the coldest biome. The average winter

Relatively little life can survive in the frigid reaches of the Arctic.

DEFINITIONS OF THE ARCTIC

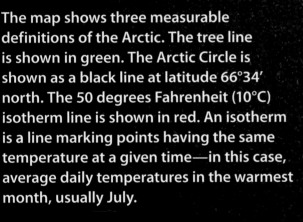

The map shows three measurable definitions of the Arctic. The tree line is shown in green. The Arctic Circle is shown as a black line at latitude 66°34′ north. The 50 degrees Fahrenheit (10°C) isotherm line is shown in red. An isotherm is a line marking points having the same temperature at a given time—in this case, average daily temperatures in the warmest month, usually July.

temperature in the tundra is -30 degrees Fahrenheit (-34°C), and the average summer temperature is 37 to 54 degrees Fahrenheit (3 to 12°C)—warm enough to support some life, but not trees.[1] The growing season is very short, at 50 to 60 days per year. Vegetation includes low shrubs, sedges, many flowers, reindeer mosses, liverworts, lichens, and grasses. The tundra also has permanently frozen soil, or permafrost.

There is no specific definition of the Arctic. It is often defined by convenience. It might include everything north of the tree line, the region where trees will no longer grow. It might include the region that has permafrost or the part of the ocean that has sea ice. Sometimes it is defined as any locations at high latitudes where average daily summer temperatures are never higher than 50 degrees Fahrenheit (10°C).[2] Sometimes, people describing the Arctic

Reindeer moss is named for the animals that eat it.

include southern regions, such as boreal forests, that do not meet other criteria for Arctic ecosystems but interact closely with them.

Within the Arctic, however it is defined, is the Arctic Circle. This is the imaginary line around Earth located at 66°34' north latitude. At this latitude, the sun does not set on the summer solstice and does not rise on the winter solstice. These two days have 24 hours of light or darkness; thus, the region around this latitude is sometimes called the land of the midnight sun. At precisely the North Pole, the sun rises only once each year and sets once each year. Technically, this means six months of daylight followed by six months of darkness. However, just as on a normal day, there are twilight periods after the sun sets and before it rises. There is a period of only approximately 11 weeks of total darkness. The number of 24-hour days and nights per season decreases when moving south from the North Pole to the Arctic Circle.

"Since October 2001, there have been no cold Octobers [in Barrow, Alaska], not one. This change is the direct result of the really catastrophic loss of autumn sea ice on Alaska's north coast."[4]

—Rick Thoman, climate sciences and service manager, NOAA, Alaska

The Arctic region has ice on both land and sea. Land ice includes glaciers, permafrost, and the largest expanse of northern ice, the Greenland ice sheet. Sea ice, or frozen ocean water, occurs in both the Arctic and Antarctic regions, and covers approximately 15 percent of the world's oceans at some time during the year.[3] Ocean water freezes at a lower temperature than freshwater due to its salt content; while freshwater freezes at 32 degrees Fahrenheit (0°C), ocean water freezes at 28.8 degrees Fahrenheit (-1.8°C). The Arctic Ocean also contains freshwater ice in the form of icebergs.

Greenland's ice sheet is enormous in scale.

LAND ICE

Land ice, or glacial ice, covers 10 percent of Earth's land area. This is a relatively small amount—during the last ice age, more than 32 percent of land was ice covered.[5] The largest portion of land ice is the two large ice sheets covering Greenland and Antarctica. Remaining land ice includes small glaciers and ice caps.

When battered by strong waves, sea ice breaks into small circular pieces called pancake ice.

All glaciers are characterized by change. They grow and shrink (advance and retreat) with changes in climate. They flow downhill because of gravity, carrying rocks, soil, and other debris with them. Glaciers are made from snow. In polar areas, more snow falls than melts during a year, so it accumulates from year to year, forming layers. The upper layers contain many air pockets and appear white. As more snow accumulates on top and deeper layers compress, more air is pressed out and the layers become increasingly denser, forming ice. The ice now appears bluish in color. This process can take more than 100 years.

Glaciers are classified by size. Small glaciers are found on mountaintops and in valleys. The largest glaciers are ice sheets. Only two ice sheets still exist on Earth—the Greenland ice sheet in the Arctic, and the Antarctic ice sheet (which really consists of two adjacent sheets) in the Southern Hemisphere. Ice sheets are huge—more than 19,300 square miles (50,000 sq km) in area.[6] When part of an ice sheet hangs out over the water and floats on it, it forms an ice shelf. When a piece of an ice shelf breaks off and enters the ocean, it becomes an iceberg. Ice caps are smaller than ice sheets.

Not all land ice in the Arctic is visible. The water in soil freezes as well, forming frozen soil called permafrost. To become permafrost, soil must remain unthawed for at least two full years. In the Northern Hemisphere, 24 percent of

WILL MELTING SEA ICE RAISE SEA LEVELS?

Most people assume that land ice melting into the oceans will raise sea levels, but melting sea ice will not. This is because sea ice is already displacing the same mass of water that it will add as it melts. But in 2005, Canadian professor Dr. Peter Noerdlinger showed that melting sea ice and ice shelves will actually add approximately 2.6 percent more water to the ocean than the amount they are displacing.[7] However, the overall effect is small. Most of the sea level rise will result from melting of land ice and thermal expansion of ocean water.

The thick layers of snow and ice near Earth's poles accumulated over the course of many years.

Photographing an entire iceberg at once is not possible, but composite photos can demonstrate how the vast majority of an iceberg's mass lies beneath the surface.

the land is covered by permafrost.[8] Some of the upper, or active, permafrost layer melts every summer, while deeper layers remain frozen.

OCEAN ICE

There are two basic types of ice in the Arctic Ocean. They are named for the way they form. Icebergs are formed from land ice, when glaciers and ice shelves calve. They are made of compacted snow, so they contain only freshwater and therefore are technically not sea ice. Most icebergs in the Arctic come from only a few sources: the northern Greenland ice sheet or Canada's Ellesmere, Baffin, and Devon Island glaciers. Approximately 90 percent of an iceberg is underwater; thus, ocean currents, rather than winds, determine their direction of travel. Icebergs formed in Greenland and Canada tend to stay in the eastern Arctic Ocean. They are eventually carried through

THE DECLINE IN ARCTIC SEA ICE

Satellites have been measuring the surface area of Arctic sea ice since 1979. This map shows the decline since then. Ice in 1980 covered the red, pink, and white areas. By 1998, it had shrunk to cover only the pink and white areas. In 2012, it was only found in the white area.

1980

1998

2012

Pack ice forms in open water and drifts with the current.

the Davis Strait (between Greenland and Baffin Island) into the Atlantic Ocean, where they melt.

The second type of Arctic Ocean ice is true sea ice, or pack ice. It is formed when seawater freezes. Approximately six feet (1.8 m) of annual pack ice forms every winter, but not all of it melts the following summer. The unmelted ice is exported via wind and ocean currents to the Atlantic, where it subsequently melts. Multiyear ice forms in the center of the ice pack, freezing in layers to the bottom of existing ice. Multiyear ice ranges in thickness from 15 to 25 feet (4.6 to 7.6 m). Individual pieces of pack ice 66 feet (20 m) or more in diameter are called ice floes. Some ice floes are small, but others are giants, more than 33,000 feet (10,000 m) wide. Unlike icebergs, ice floes are relatively flat both above and below the surface. Sometimes sea ice attaches to the shore or to some other solid structure, such as an iceberg. This attached ice is called fast ice.

Average temperatures around the world are rising due to the addition of greenhouse gases, soot, and dust to the atmosphere. This change is particularly rapid in the Arctic. According to Rick Spinrad, chief

No matter where they are emitted, greenhouse gases mix into the atmosphere and play a part in global climate change.

When ice melts, it can reveal dark rock beneath it, which can in turn accelerate warming.

scientific officer for the US National Oceanic and Atmospheric Administration (NOAA), warming in the Arctic is happening twice as fast as it is anywhere else on Earth. This is resulting in the rapid melting of Arctic ice. Before warming, much of the annual sea ice melted every summer, but older ice remained. Now, as temperatures rise, the older, thicker ice is also melting. And the melting rate is accelerating. Melting uncovers dark-colored land and water, which absorb far more heat than the white ice and snow that are lost. It is changing not only how the Arctic looks, but the processes by which it functions. This accelerated loss of Arctic ice worries many scientists, who fear it will also have increasingly serious consequences for world climate and sea level rise. Climate scientist Dr. Joe Romm warns, "We are terraforming our home planet, and the process is spinning out of control. . . . Humanity, like the Arctic, is now on very thin ice."[9]

Climate change causes melting processes to begin earlier in the year than they once did.

The effects of climate change vary from region to region; in the Arctic, they include melting ice and calving glaciers.

THREE

ARCTIC CLIMATE CHANGE

Over the past 100 years, average global temperatures have risen by approximately 1.5 degrees Fahrenheit (0.8°C). Temperatures are expected to rise anywhere between 0.5 and 8.6 degrees Fahrenheit (0.3 and 4.8°C) in the coming 100 years.[1] The variation depends on how much effort people put into controlling temperature rise. Without the most aggressive methods, temperatures will rise by at least 2.7 degrees Fahrenheit (1.5°C) by 2100.[2] The rise in global temperature causes further changes in weather and climate. These include more or less precipitation (depending on the region), which results in more floods or droughts. Changes also include more frequent and severe heat waves, more storms, and long-term changes in wind patterns.

CAUSES OF CLIMATE CHANGE

Greenhouse gases are present in very small quantities in the atmosphere. They absorb infrared radiation, or heat, and re-emit it, rather than allowing it to escape into space. This natural process, called the greenhouse effect, keeps Earth warm enough to support life. As long as amounts of greenhouse gases in the atmosphere do not change, temperatures remain relatively stable. But since the beginning of the Industrial Revolution (and especially in the last 50 to 70 years), greenhouse gas levels have been increasing rapidly as humans burn fossil fuels to produce energy. Deforestation, industrial processes, and agricultural processes also add greenhouse gases to the atmosphere.

"Climate change is already happening in the Arctic, faster than its ecosystems can adapt. Looking at the Arctic is like looking at the canary in the coal mine for the entire Earth system."[5]

—Charles Miller, NASA Jet Propulsion Laboratory, 2013

The major greenhouse gas contributing to recent climate change is carbon dioxide. It is recycled naturally through volcanic activity, exchanges with the ocean, and the respiration of living organisms. Humans add carbon dioxide by burning fossil fuels. In the 1700s, carbon dioxide levels were approximately 280 parts per million by volume (ppmv).[3] This is a measure of the number of molecules of carbon dioxide per million molecules of gas in the atmosphere. In 2016, carbon dioxide levels topped 400 ppmv and are still climbing.[4] They

Fossil fuel power plants are among the major sources of greenhouse gas emissions.

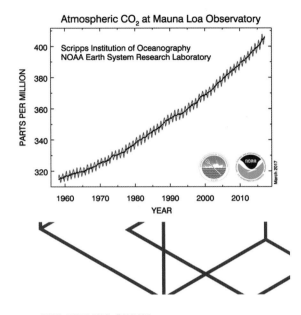

Atmospheric CO$_2$ at Mauna Loa Observatory

Scripps Institution of Oceanography
NOAA Earth System Research Laboratory

PARTS PER MILLION

400
380
360
340
320

1960   1970   1980   1990   2000   2010

YEAR

March 2017

THE KEELING CURVE

This graph, called the Keeling Curve, represents changes in atmospheric carbon dioxide levels measured at the Mauna Loa, Hawaii, measuring station. Since measurements began in 1959, values have risen from approximately 315 ppmv to more than 401 ppmv in 2016.[8] The seesaw pattern represents yearly changes as photosynthesis removes carbon dioxide in summer, and carbon dioxide levels recover in winter. The black line is the running average. This continuing rise in carbon dioxide is strongly correlated with the rise in global temperatures.

are now higher than at any time in at least 800,000 years. As of 2013, human activities were adding more than 30 billion tons (27 billion metric tons) of carbon dioxide to the atmosphere every year.[6]

Methane (CH4), the second-largest greenhouse gas source, is released by industrial, agricultural, and waste management activities. There is much less methane than carbon dioxide, but methane is more efficient at trapping heat on a per-molecule basis. Over a 100-year period, methane's heat-trapping effect is 28 to 36 times more potent than that of carbon dioxide.[7] Other greenhouse gases include nitrous oxide (N2O), water vapor, ozone, and fluoride-containing gases. Their impacts vary according to the amount present in the atmosphere, how long they remain in the atmosphere, and how strongly they absorb heat.

Greenhouse gases are not the only cause of climate change. Black carbon, or soot, is composed of solid particles produced as a by-product of burning fossil fuels, biomass, or biofuel. Black carbon in the atmosphere absorbs incoming sunlight and heat. Its major effect occurs in the Arctic, where it covers snow and ice. This causes more heat and light to be absorbed at Earth's surface and accelerates the rate of melting. Aerosols, mixtures of gases and extremely fine particles, also contribute to this process.

Climate change is also affected by the reflectivity, or albedo, of Earth's surface. Light surfaces, such as snow and clouds, reflect more sunlight, cooling the surface. Dark surfaces, such as oceans and forests, absorb more sunlight, causing warmer temperatures. Finally, the total amount of solar energy reaching Earth has some effect. But its impact on global climate is small compared to other factors, because it is relatively constant. Albedo has a far greater effect on climate.

PRESENT AND FUTURE ARCTIC CLIMATE CHANGE

The Arctic is warming faster than other parts of the world. The extent of sea ice coverage has been steadily declining over the last 30 years, reaching a record low in September 2012.[9] The melt season now lasts longer, and sea ice is becoming thinner, making it more vulnerable to continued melting. Because more ice melts every year, the remaining ice is younger and weaker.

"The Arctic ice is in a death spiral."[10]

—*Mark Serreze, National Snow and Ice Data Center*

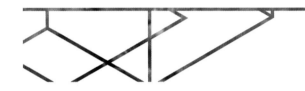

BLACK CARBON EFFECTS ON THE ARCTIC

Black carbon absorbs radiation of all wavelengths, both incoming and outgoing. (Greenhouse gases mainly trap outgoing radiation.) Absorption of incoming radiation tends to dim light at Earth's surface while warming the atmosphere. The net effect of black carbon depends on the altitude of the particles. Black carbon at high altitudes cools the surface. Most high particles enter the Arctic from industrial areas outside the region. Lower particles come from within the Arctic and cause surface warming. Black carbon deposited on ice and snow increases absorption of radiation, which speeds up melting.

THE ALBEDO EFFECT

Albedo is the reflectivity of a surface. It is measured using a number between 0 and 1. A perfectly white surface is a perfect reflector (it reflects all radiation back into space) and has an albedo of 1. A black surface is a perfect absorber (it absorbs all radiation and reflects none), and has an albedo of 0. Most surfaces are somewhere in between, but the closer the value is to 1, the higher its albedo and the more radiation it reflects. In the context of Earth, albedo is the fraction of solar radiation that reaches Earth's surface and is reflected back into space.

The albedo of open ocean water is 0.06—nearly zero. This means the ocean absorbs all but 6 percent of incoming solar radiation and becomes warmer. The albedo of bare sea ice varies from 0.5 to 0.7—that is, it reflects 50 to 70 percent of radiation. This keeps its surface much cooler. Snow-covered ice reflects (and cools) even better; its albedo is 0.9, so it reflects up to 90 percent of incoming radiation. Snow and ice, by reflecting heat, keep the surface cooler and slow the melting process. When melting finally begins and melt ponds appear on the snow surface, the surface albedo drops, eventually reaching as low as 0.15.[11]

Albedo in the Arctic is an example of a positive feedback loop, in which melting ice accelerates and amplifies warming. As ice melts, it exposes more water or land. These dark surfaces absorb more heat and speed up melting. Autumn air temperatures in the Arctic are more than 5 degrees Fahrenheit (2.75°C) higher than the long-term average. This compares to a global average temperature rise of approximately 1.5 degrees Fahrenheit (0.8°C) overall since 1880.[12]

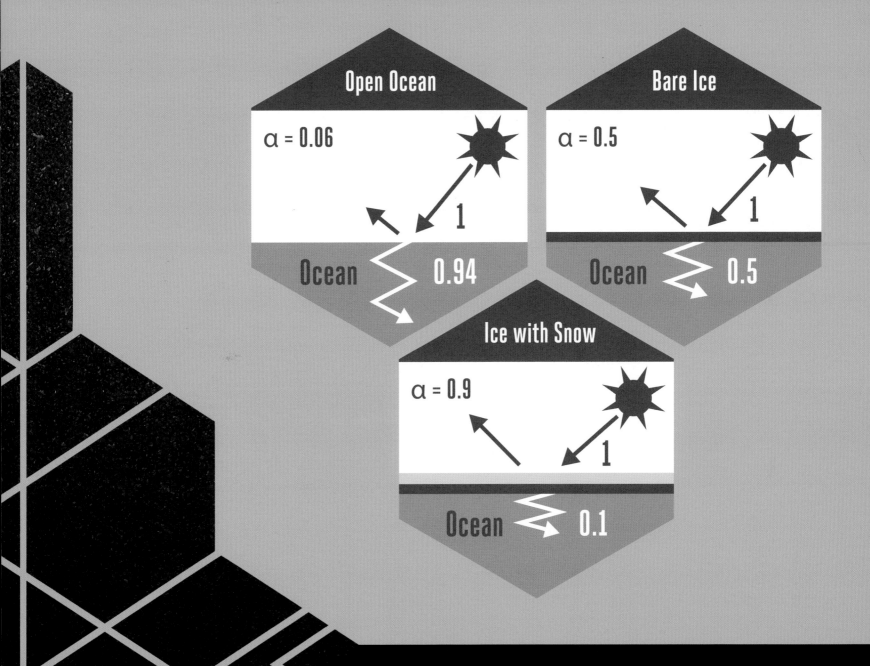

The larger an object's albedo value, the more energy is reflected off that object into space.

Land ice is also melting rapidly. In 2015, approximately 50 percent of the surface ice on the Greenland ice sheet had some summer melt.[13] This was above average, but far from a record—it was only the eleventh-highest melt in the past 37 years. Glaciers in the Arctic and elsewhere around the world show the same trends.

Melting is expected to continue at more rapid rates. Sea ice will continue to decline. On land, Arctic permafrost is already thawing, and it will thaw more in the future. This damages both infrastructure (such as buildings and pipelines) and ecosystems. Melting permafrost also releases methane, which further speeds up warming.

A major consequence of continued Arctic warming and ice melt is a rise in sea level caused by the melting of land-based glaciers and the Greenland ice sheet. According to

A house in Siberia demonstrates the damage caused by thawing and sinking permafrost.

WHEN WILL THE ICE MELT?

Lakes and rivers in the far north are melting out faster in the spring. For more than 100 years, people have held annual contests in Alaska to guess the date when river ice will break up on the Tanana and Yukon Rivers. Despite yearly variabilities, the breakup continues to occur earlier. It is now approximately one week earlier than in 1896.

the Environmental Protection Agency, sea level has risen approximately 7.5 inches (19 cm) since 1870. Scientists have projected a sea level rise of 1 to 4 feet (0.3 to 1.2 m) by 2100.[14] This rise assumes only a small input from the melting of the Antarctic ice sheets. But a new study, published in the journal *Nature* in 2016, indicates Antarctica may contribute much more. The study states that if greenhouse gas emissions continue, Antarctica's contribution could nearly double these projections of sea level rise to 6.6 feet (2 m) by 2100. This could be potentially catastrophic for low-lying coastal areas around the world.

As in the Arctic, warming temperatures are having significant effects in Antarctica.

FOUR

WHAT'S HAPPENING TO ARCTIC ICE?

I ce melt in the Arctic varies by year, season, and location. It also varies with the type of ice involved. For example, sea ice, glaciers, and ice sheets all melt in different ways. Ice melt is a process, rather than a single event. This means it would be difficult—and misleading—to give a single value for the rate of Arctic ice melt. Examining all types of melting is necessary to get a complete picture of what is happening.

Aerial views give a broad overview of the changes that Arctic ice is undergoing.

A boat navigates through countless chunks of broken-up sea ice in the Arctic Sea.

SEA ICE MEASUREMENTS

Sea ice affects cloud cover and precipitation in the Arctic. A solid cover of sea ice insulates the relatively warm Arctic Ocean from the much colder atmosphere. This insulation breaks down when the ice begins to melt and no longer forms a solid cover. Openings allow heat and water vapor to be exchanged between the ocean and atmosphere.

Scientists have made satellite measurements of Arctic ice melt since 1979. These measurements show the extent of sea ice, or the amount of surface area it covers. The values show a definite downward trend. More ice is melting, and it is melting more quickly than in the past. The months of most interest are September and March. September, at the end of summer, shows ice at its annual minimum—that is, when it has melted the most for that year. March, at the end of winter, shows ice at its annual maximum.

TRACKING SEA ICE WITH SATELLITES

Most monitoring of sea ice uses satellites that can receive data through clouds and in darkness. The first of these was launched by NASA in 1978. Scientists at the Goddard Space Flight Center and the National Snow and Ice Data Center combine all satellite data to develop data sets covering more than 30 years. The data show trends in sea ice cover from year to year. Scientists can track the ice edge and ice concentration, and they can classify different types of sea ice. Satellite data is combined with pre-satellite data from Earth-based ice charts to track Arctic ice extent since about 1900. Although earlier records are less reliable, they show that Arctic sea ice has been declining since the early 1950s.

Although the extent of sea ice is the primary measurement used by scientists, the age of the ice is also important. Older sea ice is thicker and therefore stronger. It is less likely to melt when air and water temperatures increase, or when waves and currents buffet the ice. As of 2015, the oldest Arctic ice was more than four years old. But old ice makes up less of the remaining ice each year. Much of it melts and is not replaced. In March 1985, 20 percent

SCIENCE CONNECTION

MAXIMUM AND MINIMUM FOR 2016

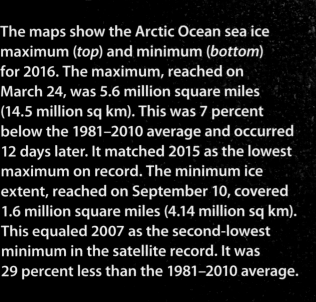

The maps show the Arctic Ocean sea ice maximum (*top*) and minimum (*bottom*) for 2016. The maximum, reached on March 24, was 5.6 million square miles (14.5 million sq km). This was 7 percent below the 1981–2010 average and occurred 12 days later. It matched 2015 as the lowest maximum on record. The minimum ice extent, reached on September 10, covered 1.6 million square miles (4.14 million sq km). This equaled 2007 as the second-lowest minimum in the satellite record. It was 29 percent less than the 1981–2010 average.

MARCH

SEPTEMBER

A Japanese scientist takes direct measurements of sea ice thickness in an Arctic region of Canada.

of the total pack ice was old ice; by March 2015, old ice had dropped to 3 percent. In 2015, 70 percent of the ice was thin first-year ice, compared to one-half that amount in 1985.[1]

Physicist and climate expert Dr. Joe Romm points out that the rapid drop in Arctic sea ice extent is accompanied by an equally rapid drop in ice thickness. This causes a decrease in ice volume. The total sea ice volume in 2016 was only approximately one-fourth its volume in 1980.[2] Walt Meier of NASA's Goddard Space Flight Center notes that sea ice is melting earlier in the year. Because

"The ice is thinner, so it gets pushed around by the wind more. It's more broken up. . . . It's like going from a big ice cube to crushed ice."[3]

—*Walt Meier, Goddard Space Flight Center, NASA*

the ice is newer and thinner, it breaks up more easily when moved by wind and waves. Rather than a solid ice pack, much of it is now chunks of ice. Within our lifetimes, some oceanographers say, the Arctic Ocean will be ice-free every summer. This will affect ocean currents and weather in Europe and the United States.

THE ANNUAL ICE CYCLE

Pre-satellite records indicate that Arctic sea ice has been declining at least since the early 1950s. Since satellite records began in 1979, total sea ice extents have declined by three percent per decade.[4] They are now declining more rapidly. Between 2002 and 2016, four new record lows were set, and several other years showed near-record lows. The ten lowest ice extents for September have all occurred since 2007.

The world's shrinking glaciers have become popular tourist attractions.

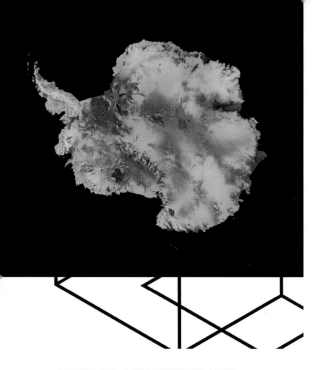

ARCTIC VS. ANTARCTIC ICE MELT

Together, the Greenland and Antarctic ice sheets contain 99 percent of Earth's freshwater ice. Most of this water is contained in the Antarctic ice sheet, which is almost 5.4 million square miles (14 million sq km) in area, approximately the size of the United States and Mexico combined.[5] It is so huge that melting of the entire Antarctic ice sheet would raise global sea level 200 feet (60 m), compared to a 20-foot (6 m) rise if the Greenland ice sheet melted.[6] Because of its size (and because it is somewhat sheltered by the cold Antarctic Ocean), the Antarctic ice sheet is melting much more slowly than the Greenland ice sheet.

The record low in 2012 was followed by four years of slightly higher ice extent. But if ice melt is increasing, why do the values not decrease every year? It is important to remember that nature is variable. Spring and summer weather conditions—for example, wind and storms that help break up the ice—can strongly affect the final percentage of ice melt. Also, circulation patterns may change. A circular pattern, or gyre, in the Beaufort Sea north of Alaska once kept ice that entered the sea in the Arctic system for years. The ice became thicker with time. But warming air temperatures and wind patterns increased ice melt in the southern part of the gyre beginning in the late 1990s. This change pushed the steep decline in ice extent and thickness.

When ice extent is measured every year and changes are plotted, the consistent downward trend becomes obvious. This rate of decrease is especially high in September. Normally, the summer ice melt would be followed by winter recovery. Ice extent and thickness would return to previous winter levels. But 2002, 2003, and 2004 were all low-ice years, and although winter recovery rates improved after 2006, winter ice extent has never returned to the 1981–2010 average. The years 2014 and 2015 tied for the record winter low: 5.6 million square miles (14.5 million sq km) of ice extent.[7]

GLACIERS AND ICE SHEETS

Movement is a key feature of all glaciers, including ice sheets. It is vital to ice melt. Glaciers flow downhill very slowly over time because of their huge weight. They also flow by a process called basal slip. The pressure and friction at a glacier's base causes a small amount of the deepest ice to melt. Top ice slides more easily over this slippery bottom layer. Now, as air temperatures increase and glacial ice melts faster, the melting ice on top forms vertical tunnels that drain meltwater to the bottom of the ice sheet. This speeds up basal slip, causing the ice sheet to move more quickly toward the ocean. Rising temperatures have caused glaciers to melt and retreat at increasingly rapid rates since the early 1900s.

The Greenland ice sheet is three times the size of Texas, or 656,000 square miles (1.7 million sq km) in area.[8] Although only

Rivers and meltwater lakes are found on Greenland's ice sheet.

A hiker stands near dense piles of firn ice.

a few meters thick at its edges, it reaches 10,500 feet (3,200 m) thick at the center.[10] Greenland's ice sheet is losing mass. Between 1979 and 2006, its summer melt increased by 30 percent, reaching a record rate in 2007.[11] New winter snow accumulates on the center of the ice sheet and has partially replaced the melt. But melt and ice calving around the edges are outpacing accumulation. Melt and glacier movement is most obvious around the edges of the glacier, where temperatures are higher and movement is faster.

Scientists have recently become aware of another factor speeding up Greenland ice melt. Firn is granular, partly compressed snow, halfway through the process of becoming ice. The firn layer is located between the top snow layers and the deeper solid ice layers. It is filled with air pockets. Until recently, scientists thought

Film crews travel to the Arctic to document the warming and melting happening there.

firn acted as a giant sponge, soaking up meltwater that trickled down from the surface and preventing it from flowing into the ocean. But a recent study showed that meltwater passes through the firn and, when it reaches a solid ice layer, drains into the ocean.

The Arctic is warming twice as fast as the rest of the planet. As a result, both sea ice and glacial ice are melting rapidly. Melting ice and other impacts of climate change will be felt beyond the Arctic. They will affect global climate, sea level, and biodiversity of ecosystems, not to mention the Arctic people and the economies of human cultures around the world.

FIVE

MELTING ICE AND CHANGING ECOSYSTEMS

C limate change and Arctic ice melt are changing ecosystems on land and at sea. For better or worse, the Arctic will look considerably different in the coming years. Rising temperatures not only melt ice, they also cause some

Polar bears are among the many organisms affected by climate change and Arctic melting.

STUDYING ICE ALGAE

Craig Aumack of Columbia University heads a team studying sea ice algae in Alaska. The scientists travel across the ice on snowmobiles. They are accompanied by a guide and a bear guard, who protects them from polar bears. They drill cores of ice down to the water and measure their length. They construct a temperature profile by measuring temperature every 3.9 inches (10 cm).[4] Then they study the section closest to the water. In the lab, they melt the ice slowly and retrieve the organisms. They identify the algae and the algae eaters and construct food webs for this icy community.

plants and animals from farther south to migrate north, either displacing or living among native Arctic species. Some Arctic species might be unable to adapt to changing conditions and die out.

THE RISE OF ARCTIC ALGAE

As sea ice thins and more light penetrates, large deposits of dense ice algae are now growing from the bottoms of ice floes throughout the Arctic. Many are growing on ice only approximately three feet (1 m) thick. They also carpet the ocean floor in many areas. This lush algal growth probably results from sunlight pouring through meltwater ponds covering the surface of the newer, thinner ice floes. According to oceanographer C. J. Mundy, "The ponds are like windows to let light through the sea ice."[1] They transmit approximately half the amount of light available at the surface. Older, thicker ice has smaller melt ponds, which cover less surface area and allow less light to penetrate.

Ice algae currently make up 3 to 25 percent of all marine primary producers (algae or phytoplankton, which form the base of the food chain) in the Arctic, and more than 50 percent

Algae grow on the underside of sea ice.

in high Arctic regions with more ice.[2] As ice thins and they receive more light, ice algae will increase at first, but as continued warming melts the ice, they will have less habitat and begin to die out. This will cause a shift from ice algae to pelagic (floating) phytoplankton as the major primary producers. This in turn will affect the types and numbers of zooplankton that feed on them.

ARCTIC OCEAN ACIDIFICATION

Carbon dioxide dissolving in the ocean has two separate effects. First, it forms carbonic acid, which increases ocean acidity. The cold waters of the Arctic acidify very easily, because cold water absorbs more carbon dioxide than warmer water. Higher acid levels harm animals that build shells, such as sea snails and mussels. Slightly increased acid makes shells weaker; higher levels dissolve them. Second, carbon dioxide is a raw material for photosynthesis. When ocean phytoplankton die or are consumed, some of their photosynthesized carbon falls to the deep ocean sediments. This removes it from the atmosphere and slows global warming. But there is a catch. Excess carbon dioxide causes tiny phytoplankton to reproduce more rapidly and produce more total biomass than larger phytoplankton. But larger phytoplankton are more efficient at moving carbon to ocean depths, and their mass is decreasing when it is most needed.

ARCTIC OCEAN FOOD WEBS

Oceans make up more than one-half of Arctic surface area, and many large Arctic animals depend on the oceans and sea ice for survival. Polar bears hunt, give birth, and travel on sea ice. They lie in wait on the ice for seals, their major food source. Some seal species live all or most of their lives on sea ice. They feed, rest, give birth, and raise pups on the ice. Walruses use the edges of sea ice as diving platforms to feed on clams on the ocean floor. But now, some female and baby walruses in Alaska are traveling as much as 110 miles (180 km) to reach land instead, according to Kit Kovacs of the Norwegian Polar Institute.[5] As sea ice continues to melt and recede, all of these animals have less habitat, less access to food, and a lower likelihood of survival.

Certain kinds of seabirds are also feeling the loss of sea ice. Ivory gulls nest on rocky cliffs on the coast, but they fly out onto sea ice to feed. They fish through cracks in the ice and follow polar bears to scavenge their kills. They depend not only on the amount of ice available, but also on the length of the ice season—that is, when the ice melts, reforms, and melts again. As sea ice has declined and ice seasons have shortened in the last several decades, ivory gull populations in Canada have declined by 70 to 80 percent.[6]

LAND ECOSYSTEMS IN THE ARCTIC

Land-based food webs vary depending on the depth of permafrost. In northern Alaska, above the Brooks Range of mountains, permafrost is continuous and reaches as deep as 1,300 feet (396 m). But farther south, unfrozen surface soil begins to occur. Where there is at least four feet (1.2 m) of soil above the permafrost, trees including white spruce, birch, cottonwood, and some willows begin to grow. Where there is less than 18 inches (0.5 m) of soil above the permafrost, the only trees are black spruce.[7] Most vegetation consists of wild cranberries, blueberries, mosses, and lichens. This vegetation helps insulate and maintain permafrost. Continued warming,

"Like the predictions for polar bears, recent declines in ivory gull populations may be a harbinger of the future for ice-associated species in the Arctic."[8]

—N. C. Spencer, H. G. Gilchrist, and M. L. Mallory, PLOS One, 2014

HOW POLAR BEARS ARE COPING WITH CLIMATE CHANGE

As Arctic sea ice melts, polar bears are less able to capture seals, their major food source. With less food, polar bear numbers are dwindling rapidly. To ward off starvation, they are developing new behaviors. Bears off Svalbard, Norway, were observed eating a dolphin and burying the leftovers in the ice. In Canada, some polar bears eat snow goose eggs as a backup food source. As the summer melting season lengthens, polar bears are spending more time on shore. Bears near human settlements are even foraging for human food. Although polar bears are trying hard to stay alive, none of these behaviors will ultimately keep them from starving as the ice melts.

which leads to more forest fires and insect outbreaks, will melt permafrost faster. Black spruce relies on permafrost to maintain stable roots. However, the melting is often sporadic, or spotty. This causes the trees to lean in different directions. As warming proceeds, the growth of these trees will be impaired. Many of them eventually topple.

When permafrost is deep and continuous, the base of the tundra food web includes grasses, mosses, and lichens. But repeated freezing and thawing of shallow permafrost forms an ice crust that prevents grazing and damages or kills these plants. This destroys the food and habitat of lemmings and voles, and their populations decline. Their predators, including snowy owls, weasels, and ermine, then have less food and also begin to decline. If lemming populations get too low, some predators switch to other prey.

Black spruce trees are vulnerable to warming in their ecosystem.

The Peary caribou is the smallest subspecies of caribou.

For example, Arctic foxes begin to prey on wading birds. This lowers wading bird populations. In general, warming leads to simpler ecosystems with lower biodiversity. With fewer species at each level of the food web, the loss or decline of a single species quickly affects the entire web.

Over the past few decades, lemmings, musk oxen, and caribou have had population crashes. For example, Peary caribou depend on sea ice to travel among the 36,000 islands in the Canadian archipelago. As the ice vanishes, they have more difficulty mating, raising young, and finding food and shelter. Because they have fewer choices of mates, genetic diversity in caribou populations is declining. This could eventually lead to their extinction. Northward movement of some plant and animal species will also affect caribou and other populations. As tundra vegetation and trees shift northward, this reduces the amount of tundra available for grazing. Caribou herds rely on tundra vegetation, particularly during the calving season.

THE CHANGING ARCTIC TUNDRA BIOME
Climate change is causing changes in Arctic vegetation in some regions. The biome in these regions—for example, at the tree line in the western Canadian Arctic—is "greening." It is becoming more productive and has greater biomass. However, the vegetation is different. Typical tundra vegetation is being replaced by more southern vegetation from the boreal forest. Here, shrubs, including tall shrubs such as alder, are expanding northward from forest edges into adjacent tundra. The International Tundra Experiment (ITEX), a collaborative project involving scientists from 11 nations, has documented increases in canopy height and dominance of shrubs. Warming experiments indicate that, in the future, some parts of the tundra will show changes in species composition and abundance, and decreases in diversity.

Also, as winter temperatures increase by 10.8 degrees Fahrenheit (6°C) by the end of the current century, the number of freeze-thaw cycles on land is expected to increase.[9] Ground covered in ice, caused by more freezing rain, can hinder the ability of caribou both to find food and to raise calves, causing declines in their numbers. This in turn will greatly affect indigenous human populations, which depend on caribou for food, shelter, tools, fuel, and other items.

Warming will have significant negative effects on the Arctic's large caribou herds, as well as on the people that rely on them.

SCIENCE CONNECTION

PERMAFROST AND ACCELERATING MELT

Arctic permafrost stores more than one trillion short tons (0.9 trillion metric tons) of carbon—more than twice as much as in the atmosphere.[10] Permafrost is now a carbon sink. But as Arctic temperatures warm, permafrost melts and releases its stored carbon, mostly in the form of methane. Methane, like carbon dioxide, is a heat-trapping greenhouse gas. Although it stays in the atmosphere for a much shorter time than carbon dioxide, it is a much more potent greenhouse gas. Over a 100-year period, methane will absorb 35 times more heat per molecule than carbon dioxide.[11] When released into the atmosphere, methane sets up a positive feedback loop that amplifies global warming. Scientists expect this process to speed up. By the mid-2020s, the tundra could be releasing more carbon than it is storing.

But it is difficult to determine how much methane is being released. Methane comes from different areas over the Arctic and from different sources. Sometimes, when permafrost thaws, the soil collapses, forming

thaw lakes. Methane bubbles up rapidly from thaw lakes. In other areas, permafrost thaws to form fens and bogs. These marshy areas have high concentrations of peat, and both produce methane.

Scientists are not sure how much additional warming melting permafrost might cause. But a 2015 study suggests the amount will be significant. According to Ted Schuur of Northern Arizona University, "The permafrost carbon . . . will seep out slowly in small amounts in a very large number of places."[12] By 2100, this methane seepage could add the equivalent of 60 to 80 ppmv of carbon dioxide to the atmosphere. Atmospheric carbon dioxide is already expected to be about 800 ppmv (twice the 2015 level), which would raise temperatures 8.6 degrees Fahrenheit (4.7°C) above 1986–2005 temperatures. Permafrost melt would raise greenhouse gas levels another 10 percent, and would raise temperatures accordingly.[13]

The melting and refreezing cycles of permafrost can give the
ground a distinctive bumpy look.

SIX

MELTING ICE AND ARCTIC PEOPLE

C hanges in the Arctic due to rising temperatures and melting ice will eventually affect everyone in the world. But the greatest and most immediate changes will be to the indigenous Arctic people, such as the Inuits of North America. Melting permafrost will endanger infrastructure and impede transportation, while other changes will occur in the transport of and access to the rich resources of the Arctic.

Urpignak, an Inuit man, digs into the Arctic ice to collect mussels.

EFFECTS ON INDIGENOUS PEOPLE

Arctic people living close to the coast face a combination of melting, erosion, sea level rise, and violent storms. Melting ice and warmer temperatures add moisture to the atmosphere, which increases formation of storms. It also allows larger waves to reach the shore. Thus, storm surges crash into, erode, and damage Arctic coastlines. This is forcing people to relocate. The protective break walls of the coastal village of Nelson Lagoon, Alaska, have been repeatedly destroyed by storms. Erosion around Shishmaref, Alaska (north of Nome), threatens homes, water systems, and other infrastructure. In summer 2016, the people of Shishmaref voted to evacuate and relocate, as sea ice and coastal permafrost continued to melt. Some buildings, including cultural and archaeological sites, have already

Fishers work in Tuktoyaktuk, a community that has been significantly affected by climate change.

TREKKING THE CHANGING ARCTIC

In early 2007, a polar exploration team headed by Will Steger trekked 1,000 miles (1,600 km) across Baffin Island, in the Canadian province of Nunavut.[2] The group traveled with three Inuit hunter guides and a dogsled team. Steger wanted to see the effects of climate change on Inuit people at the Arctic edge. Among other things, the team saw that Inuits now have fewer hunting days per year and more difficulty building igloos. For generations, they have used specific ice formations as landmarks, but shifting winds have made these formations unrecognizable. Steger's team crossed ice caps, frozen rivers, thawing ice, and fjords. The group ended at the Inuit town of Iglulik, whose 1,600 inhabitants welcomed them with fire trucks, lights, and air raid sirens. The 4,000-year-old town, whose name means "home to the igloo people," is the cultural center of Nunavut.[3]

been destroyed in Tuktoyaktuk, Canada. This site may soon be uninhabitable.

Sea ice is now both thinner and farther from shore, making it more difficult for hunters to travel. Hunters in Shishmaref must now travel 200 miles (322 km) from their coastal town to hunt walruses.[1] Seal hunters must hunt seals by boat, instead of over the ice. The changes in sea ice (thinning, cracking, and changing dates of ice freezing and breakup) also make hunting less safe. Accidents and deaths on the ice, the loss of expensive equipment, and stranded hunting parties are becoming more common.

Indigenous people across the Arctic are documenting climate-related changes in their lives. For example, they are now often unable to predict weather as accurately as in the past. They see less snow and more freezing rain in autumn and winter. This makes it more difficult to build the igloos they use on hunting trips. They even see some extreme heat in summers. The ice cellars in which they have always stored food are melting. New species of fish and birds are appearing—salmon, barn owls, and robins, among others. Black flies and mosquitoes are invading. According to Sheila Watt-Cloutier, chair of the Inuit Circumpolar Conference, "Climate change is not just a theory to us in the Arctic, it is a stark and dangerous reality. Human-induced climate change is undermining the ecosystem upon which Inuit depend for their cultural survival. The Arctic is not wilderness or a frontier, it is our home."[4]

EFFECTS FROM THE INDUSTRIALIZED WORLD

Eight countries have land surrounding the Arctic: Denmark, Norway, Sweden, Iceland, Finland, Canada, Russia, and the United States. Greenland is a part of the Kingdom of Denmark, but it has its own political system. These eight nations together account for 40 percent of the world's greenhouse gas emissions.[5] Thus, while parts of these nations suffer from the effects of climate change, their industrial activities cause much of the problem. Increasingly, research suggests that the Arctic serves as a bellwether, or a canary in the coal mine. That is, what happens first in the Arctic will soon be seen in the rest of the world.

"People further south on the globe go to the supermarket, Inuit go on the sea-ice. . . . When they can no longer hunt what is on the sea-ice their entire existence as a people is threatened."[6]

—*Sheila Watt-Cloutier, Chair of the Inuit Circumpolar Conference*

For the people who live in the Arctic, climate change and melting are already having noticeable effects.

EXCESS ULTRAVIOLET RADIATION

Greenhouse gases trap heat and raise temperatures, leading to climate change. A completely different group of gases, called CFCs, help deplete the ozone layer, letting more ultraviolet radiation reach Earth's surface. Ozone depletion is severe in the Arctic, and it is strongly influenced by temperature changes. An international treaty, the Montreal Protocol, took effect in 1989 and banned the input of more CFCs into the atmosphere. But those already released have long life-spans. The Arctic will suffer from increased levels of ultraviolet radiation for several more decades. Excess ultraviolet radiation has serious effects on humans, including skin cancer, sunburn, cataracts, cornea damage, and suppression of the immune system. It stresses ecosystems and damages plastics and other building materials.

Developed countries already exploit Arctic resources. In the past, sea ice has made accessing these resources difficult. But melting ice opens up new shipping routes and lengthens the shipping season. Soon, there will likely be more conflicts among competing countries for access to Arctic resources, including fish, seals, and marine wildlife, as well as more tourism. Commercial interests will compete with each other and with indigenous people for these resources. More services such as ice breaking, ice charting, and emergency response to disasters will be needed. Shipping may become easier as ice melts and breaks up. However, it will not necessarily be safer or more predictable, because the amount of ice and its movement varies from year to year.

A major Arctic resource is oil. The greatest risk from oil exploration and removal is environmental damage due to oil spills and industrial accidents. The environmental effects of oil spills are much worse in the Arctic than at lower latitudes, because the cold environment prevents breakdown of pollutants. The *Exxon Valdez* oil tanker spill occurred in March 1989 in Alaska's Prince William Sound. It killed thousands of seabirds and marine mammals and forced the closure of commercial fisheries and areas where wild foods were harvested. In 2014, on the

The *Exxon Valdez* incident highlighted the fragility of Arctic ecosystems.

ALASKA BATTLES MELTING PERMAFROST

South of the Brooks Range of mountains in Alaska, permafrost is melting. As it melts, the water flows away and the ground sinks—not evenly, but with dips and troughs. This is a challenge for the Alaska Department of Transportation and Public Facilities. Mike Coffey, chief of maintenance and operations, has worked in Fairbanks for 32 years. In the past, he says, fall temperatures fell suddenly to below 0 degrees Fahrenheit (-18°C) and stayed there until spring. Now, there are constant freeze-thaw cycles, which cause icy roads when meltwater refreezes. In the summers, Coffey says, "we're removing pavement, re-leveling, . . . then repaving or chip sealing back over the top to try to smooth roads out."[9] In winter, they are doing anti-icing treatments for the first time.

twenty-fifth anniversary of the oil spill, pockets of oil from it were still being found along the Alaskan coast.

EFFECTS ON LAND

On land, thawing permafrost is a serious problem for transportation and industrial activities. Travel on the tundra is easier in winter because the frozen ground can support ice roads and bridges. When permafrost melts and the ground becomes mushy, travel is much more difficult. Thirty years ago, travel over the tundra was possible more than 200 days per year. By 2016, due to melting, this had declined to only 100 days per year.[7] This means heavy equipment, including that used in oil and gas exploration and extraction, can be used only half as much as previously. Forestry also suffers as permafrost melts. There is a shorter period every year during which timber and finished wood can be transported.

Infrastructure as well as transportation is suffering. In Alaska, melting permafrost is causing houses to tilt on their foundations or sink into the ground. Residents on hillsides have their wells run dry as permafrost melts; those downhill have basements filled with water. New construction of buildings

The melting of permafrost can have drastic effects on paved roads and other infrastructure.

and industrial facilities is becoming more expensive because buildings require deeper foundations. Northern Russia is suffering damage to railroad lines, airport runways, and oil and gas pipelines as permafrost thaws. There is also fear that future melting might lead to groundwater contamination if the walls of open-pit mines collapse and release mine waste. Such infrastructure problems will continue until all permafrost melts, which will likely take centuries.

Ecosystem changes in the Arctic, as well as changes to transport and infrastructure, are inevitable as warming continues. The Arctic people live with these changes every day, and they are determined to adapt with them.

SEVEN

MELTING ICE AND RISING SEA LEVELS

T he Arctic is warming twice as fast as anywhere else on Earth. In October 2016, Arctic temperatures were 36 degrees Fahrenheit (20°C) warmer than average for that month.[1] This record high tops records just set in 2014 and 2015. According to Rick Thoman, NOAA's climate science and services manager for Alaska, there was "a meteoric rise in

The melting of Greenland's ice sheet is projected to contribute to significant sea level rises.

October temperatures on Alaska's north slope."[2] Arctic sea ice in October 2016 reached a record low of 28.5 percent below the average for 1981–2010.

Greenland's ice sheet is also melting much faster than scientists predicted. This is not due to an increased rate of global warming, but because scientists now understand the melting process better. They think much of the ice sheet's surface meltwater is entering the ocean immediately, rather than being absorbed again deeper within the ice sheet, as previously thought. Meltwater from the Greenland ice sheet plus that from smaller land glaciers and ice caps is responsible for rising sea levels around the world. Icebergs formed when chunks of ice break off the Greenland ice sheet and flow into the ocean also add to rising sea levels. Rising sea levels are perhaps the most serious and long-lasting impact of melting Arctic ice.

WHAT IS SEA LEVEL RISE?

Global temperatures have risen 1.4 degrees Fahrenheit (0.8°C) in the past 100 years, and global sea level has risen approximately eight inches (20 cm) since 1880. Although eight inches seems like a very small rise, it is highly significant for several reasons. First, this is an average value. In some places, the rise has been small and not noticeable, but in others, it has been much higher and has already caused serious damage. Second, it is just the beginning. The rate of sea level rise is accelerating. Past greenhouse gas emissions that have built up in the atmosphere are currently speeding up warming. The momentum of this warming will cause sea levels to rise for decades, regardless of humans' future actions.

Third, although human actions in the coming decades cannot stop this rise, they can control its rate by controlling the level of greenhouse gases entering the atmosphere.

According to the National Ocean Service, the rate of sea level rise since 1992 has been 1.2 inches (3 cm) per decade.[3] This is significantly larger than any rate for the past 2,000 years. If all greenhouse gas emissions had stopped in 2016, sea levels would still rise between 1.2 and 2.6 feet (0.4-0.8 m) by 2100, due to already existing greenhouse gases.[4] Since emissions did not stop in 2016, the rise will be higher than this. Depending on future greenhouse gas emissions, sea levels could rise as much as 6.6 feet (2 m) above the 1992 levels.[5] If the oceans and atmosphere continue to warm, sea levels will rise for many centuries at rates higher than in the present century.

IMPACTS OF SEA LEVEL RISE

In the United States, more than one-third of the population, or more than 100 million people, lives in counties along the coasts.[6] In the 1900s, sea level rise occurred fastest along the US East Coast and the Gulf of Mexico. States with the most low-lying land include Florida, Louisiana, North and South

"We must prepare for rising seas _and_ work to limit the long-term pace and magnitude of sea level rise by dramatically reducing global warming emissions."[7]
—_Union of Concerned Scientists_

WHY SEA LEVEL RISES

Sea level rise has two major causes. One is melted land ice (from glaciers, ice caps, and ice sheets) that flows into the sea. The second is thermal expansion, or the increase in water volume as the water warms. Ocean water is warming rapidly, as it absorbs more than 90 percent of the heat associated with global warming.[8] From the beginning of the Industrial Revolution in 1760 until about 1880, thermal expansion was the major cause of rising sea levels. But as melting of land ice has increased, it has contributed more. Between 1972 and 2008, melting was responsible for 52 percent of the rise; warmer oceans contributed 38 percent, and 10 percent came from other sources. Melting has accelerated since the early 1990s, and since 2003, it has caused 75 to 80 percent of the increase.[9]

Vast numbers of people live just above sea level on the Florida coastline.

Carolina, and California. In the coming years, these states (and others with low-lying land) can expect at least four major impacts from rising sea levels: erosion and deterioration of shorelines as ocean waters reach farther inland; floods caused by storm surges pushing farther inland, damaging or destroying homes and infrastructure; flooding that does not recede, much of which will occur in Florida; and saltwater contamination of fresh groundwater, which is used for drinking and agriculture.

Officials in the Maldives, an island nation at severe risk from sea level rise, held an underwater meeting to highlight the danger climate change poses to their country.

The effects of sea level rise will be much worse for other countries than for the United States. Many of these countries are extremely poor. They have little money to improve infrastructure, deal with floods and related disasters, or move endangered people away from coasts. According to Climate Central, of the 20 countries most at risk from sea level rise, the top seven (and 12 of the 20) are in Asia.[10] They include China, Vietnam, Japan, India, and Bangladesh. Another five are in Europe. The other three are the United States, Brazil, and Nigeria. The United States is eleventh on the list.

ISLAND EVACUATIONS ARE UNDER WAY

The world's first official climate refugees left their home in the Carteret Islands of Papua New Guinea in 2009. Rising tides had washed away or poisoned their crops with saltwater. The small island's 2,000 people moved to another, larger island on higher ground. Tuvalu, a tiny island between Hawaii and Australia, is experiencing contaminated drinking water, lower food production, and erosion as it floods more each year. Tuvalu has asked both Australia and New Zealand to accept its 11,000 inhabitants as climate refugees, but neither has agreed. The Pacific Island of Kiribati is also making plans to evacuate. Its government recently purchased a section of another island 1,200 miles (2,000 km) away in Fiji. The government plans to develop the land for agriculture and fish farming. It will become a refuge for Kiribati's 103,000 residents as rising sea levels submerge their island within the next two to three decades.[12]

Large cities will suffer both physical and financial losses. According to the World Bank, five of the ten largest cities that will flood as climate change continues are in the United States. They include (in order of risk) Miami, Florida; New York, New York; New Orleans, Louisiana; Tampa, Florida; and Boston, Massachusetts. Miami is most at risk because it is already at sea level. The other five cities are in China, India, and Japan. If coastal cities fail to adapt, the World Bank, an international financial organization, calculates that flood damages could reach $1 trillion per year. It projects that average global flood losses will increase from $6 billion per city in 2005 to $52 billion in 2050, based on increasing population and property values.[11] The poor in all cities will be most at risk. As cities grow, poorer residents are forced into low-lying neighborhoods more vulnerable to flooding. All forms of infrastructure will be at risk as sea levels rise. These include roads, bridges, subways, water supplies, power plants, sewage-treatment plants, oil and gas wells, and landfills. As these flood, they will impact jobs, industries, and people's everyday lives.

Sea level rise at specific locations will vary drastically. One factor influencing the amount of rise (in addition to Arctic melting) is the sinking of land. Sometimes land sinks due to natural processes, but human activities such as withdrawing groundwater and fossil fuels also cause sinking.

OTHER EFFECTS OF ARCTIC MELTING

Sea level rise is the most obvious global change resulting from the melting Arctic. But it is not the only one. The ice-albedo effect is a positive feedback loop that accelerates the rate of warming as melting ice decreases albedo and increases heat absorption. This speeds up Arctic melting, and thereby speeds up all the factors it affects—including rising sea levels. *National Geographic* writer Peter Miller points to the unpredictable effects of melting sea ice on climate. Melting sea ice raises Arctic temperatures, as the dark ocean absorbs more heat. These changes alter the polar front jet stream, a narrow river of westerly winds several miles above Earth. The jet

Ordinarily, bright white sea ice reflects some of the sun's energy back into space, regulating Earth's temperature.

THE MELTING ANTARCTIC

The Antarctic ice sheets have the greatest potential to raise sea levels. Antarctica has 90 percent of the world's ice, with ice sheets averaging 7,000 feet (2,100 m) thick. A 2016 study has almost doubled projected estimates of sea level rise due to Antarctic melting. In the worst case, sea levels could rise almost four feet (1.2 m) by 2100.[13] This would submerge parts of New Orleans; Miami Beach, Florida; the Florida Keys; and many East Coast cities.

stream changes weather patterns—when it dips farther south, that area has a cold wave; when it remains farther north, weather in the south remains warm. Such changes make future weather conditions uncertain.

Rising seas will make life more difficult in developing nations, where people often rely on the ocean's present state for their livelihoods.

MELTING ICE AND THE OCEAN CONVEYOR BELT

Melting sea ice can also affect world climate through the ocean's thermohaline circulation. *Thermo-* refers to temperature and *-haline* to salinity, or saltiness. The combination of temperature and salinity of water determines its horizontal and vertical movement. When sea ice forms, the water freezes but the salt stays behind, making the remaining water more saline. This salty water is dense, so it sinks. This helps drive a worldwide circulation pattern—the ocean conveyor belt. Wind drives the surface currents. The conveyor belt carries warm water from the equator to the poles and cold water back toward the equator, where the cycle repeats. In the diagram, blue arrows indicate the path of cold, dense water currents flowing deep in the ocean. Red arrows show warmer, less dense surface currents.

Climate change is slowing the ocean conveyor belt. When warm water reaches the northern ocean, it cools, releasing its heat into the atmosphere. The cold water sinks, and warm water moves in to replace it. This occurs most easily in gyres, or circular currents, in the Greenland Sea and the Iceland Sea. But two factors are currently weakening this sinking process. First, melting ice from Greenland is adding freshwater to the Atlantic. The less dense freshwater does not sink as deeply. Second, heat transfer is much less efficient. Efficient heat transfer requires a large difference between water and air temperature. With sea ice melting and retreating north, there is less ice near the gyres, making temperature differences smaller and producing less salty, dense water. Since 1979, heat loss has decreased by 20 percent.[14]

As the ocean conveyor belt slows, less heat will reach Europe, which could cool the continent or warm it more slowly. Also, if the ocean conveyor belt weakens, North American waters could warm and expand. This would cause more rapid sea level rise along the east coast of North America. Scientists are not yet certain of the effects of a weakened ocean conveyor belt.

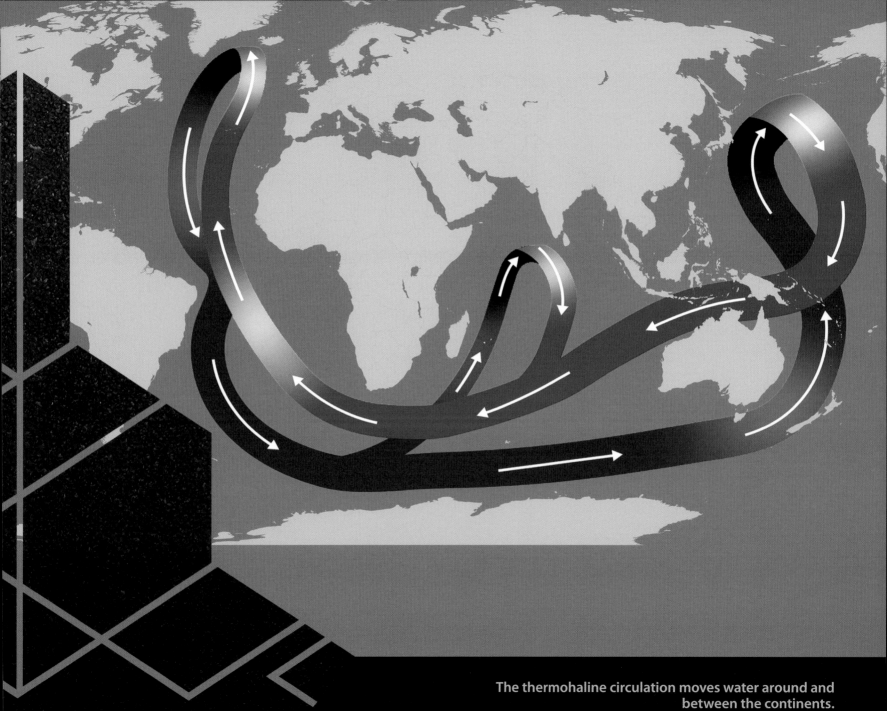

The thermohaline circulation moves water around and between the continents.

EIGHT

CAN THE MELTING BE STOPPED?

The ultimate cause of melting ice in the Arctic is global warming. This results from greenhouse gases emitted mostly by fossil fuel burning, and it is a global problem. Annual summits are held by the Conference of the Parties (COP), a group of nations, to urge world political leaders to work together on solutions. One of these resulted in the Paris Agreement, reached at the COP21 summit in 2015. Leaders

US secretary of state John Kerry spoke at the United Nations signing ceremony for the Paris Agreement.

THE FUTURE OF GLOBAL WARMING

Global temperatures rise when atmospheric greenhouse gas concentrations rise. Thus, cutting global greenhouse gas emissions is the only sure way to slow rising temperatures and Arctic ice melt. International authorities have studied four pathways for cutting greenhouses gas emissions (called Representative Concentration Pathways, or RCPs), and the corresponding global temperatures in which these levels would result. The lowest emissions (RCP 2.6) result in the lowest temperature increase, a rise of approximately 1.8 degrees Fahrenheit (1°C). The highest emissions (RCP 8.5) result in a global rise of more than 7.2 degrees Fahrenheit (4°C). Projected changes are relative to the 1986–2005 average, and would occur before 2100.[3]

agreed to keep global temperature rise during this century below 3.6 degrees Fahrenheit (2°C) above preindustrial levels. They hope to limit the rise to only 2.7 degrees Fahrenheit (1.5°C).[1] To do this, countries must limit their emissions of carbon dioxide and other greenhouse gases. With appropriate use of money and technology, signers of the agreement also plan to help poorer countries deal with the impacts of climate change. To finalize the agreement, 112 of the 197 participating countries had to ratify it. This goal was reached on October 5, 2016, and the Paris Agreement went into effect on November 4, 2016.

WHAT IF CLIMATE CHANGE IS NOT SLOWED DOWN?

Many experts say crossing the 3.6° F (2°C) limit would result in a grim future for humanity. Scott Barrett, an economist from Columbia University, says, "The more the mean temperature rises, the more you're moving away from a system that we've been comfortable with and that has been stable for 10,000 years. It's the things that would be triggered by the change in temperature that would matter."[2] These include famine, extreme weather events, and the breaking up of the Greenland and Antarctic ice sheets—leading to massive sea level rises. Already, since 2008, 22.5 million people worldwide have

Large sea level rises over the next few centuries could threaten New York City's Manhattan Island.

lost their homes every year because of extreme weather. By 2030, an additional 250,000 per year could die as a result of malnutrition, disease, and heat stress driven by climate change.[4]

Princeton University geoscientist Michael Oppenheimer says that, over the next two to three centuries, sea levels could rise up to 40 feet (12 m) from melting at both poles.[5] Before 2050, US regions including South Florida; Norfolk, Virginia; New York City; and New Orleans will be hard hit. Oppenheimer says short-term sea level rise is likely to be faster than anything humanity has seen before.

To stabilize the climate, greenhouse gas levels in the atmosphere must stabilize. Given that some greenhouse gases last for thousands of years, this means their emissions must go to zero. This in turn means eliminating fossil fuels and replacing them with alternative energy sources that do not release greenhouse gases. Many experts think it is already too late to reach the 3.6° F (2°C) target. Barrett says simple math shows that global emissions will rise through 2030, even if all countries fulfill their pledges to decrease greenhouse gas emissions. According to Oppenheimer, greenhouse gas emissions must reach zero by somewhere around mid-century—2050 or perhaps 2060—to meet the target temperature.

Still, many people in the United States and in the world do not see climate change as a serious problem. A 2015 poll from National Public Radio and the Pew Research Center showed that 30 percent of Americans and 40 percent of people worldwide do not think they will be impacted by climate change.[6] In late 2015, the US House of Representatives blocked an attempt to cut the amount of greenhouse gases released by US power plants. Every year of delay means another 40 billion tons (36 billion metric tons) of carbon dioxide entering the atmosphere—and warming it.[7]

Electric cars may be one part of the solution to cutting carbon emissions, especially if they use electricity generated by renewable sources.

GLOBAL WARMING SOLUTIONS

The Union of Concerned Scientists states that we already have the technology and practical solutions to combat and significantly slow global warming. These climate solutions include:

» Using more renewable energy and making our energy system cleaner and less fossil fuel dependent.

» Increasing vehicle fuel efficiency and supporting other means of reducing US oil use.

» Limiting the amount of carbon polluters can emit.

» Investing in energy-efficient technologies, industries, and methods.

» Reducing tropical deforestation, which increases greenhouse gas emissions.

PLANET ENGINEERING—REFREEZING THE ARCTIC

According to David Keith, a professor of applied physics at Harvard University, we could combat ice melting by refreezing the Arctic. Injecting reflective particles into the upper atmosphere would reduce the amount of sunlight reaching the surface and counteract the greenhouse effect. Although high greenhouse gas levels would continue to trap heat, surface temperatures would go down because less energy would reach the surface. Reducing solar energy input by only 0.5 percent in the Arctic could restore sea ice to pre-industrial levels. Keith thinks this method should be used only in a "climate emergency," such as a sudden ice sheet collapse or a killing drought.[9] We should research all possible solutions, Keith says, but the best approach is to reduce greenhouse gas emissions.

What is missing from this list may be the political will to accomplish it. In 2013, President Barack Obama outlined a national climate action plan that included limits on carbon emissions from power plants, improved efficiency standards for buildings and appliances, and increased use of renewable energy. But he met an almost complete lack of support in Congress. Whether the US government takes action or not, alternative energy technologies such as wind and solar will become cheaper and eventually overcome fossil fuels. Electric vehicles will continue to improve until internal combustion cars are considered old-fashioned. In short, the switchover to clean energy will continue, although much more slowly than if the United States were leading the transition.

Dr. Paul Salaman, a conservationist with the Rainforest Trust, makes a strong case for fighting climate change—and saving Arctic ice—by saving and replanting rainforest trees. Although he acknowledges that cutting carbon emissions is essential, Salaman points out that rainforest conservation could be half of the solution to global warming. While cutting carbon emissions would put less carbon into the atmosphere, adding to rainforests would pull more carbon out of the atmosphere and store it in the trees. This would provide an immediate reduction in atmospheric carbon dioxide, which would increase as the trees grow. In addition, rainforest conservation costs very little. An acre of Amazon rainforest in Peru can be protected for just a few dollars, and it stores up to 198 short tons (180 metric tons) of carbon dioxide.[10]

"The really hard questions here aren't mostly technical. They're questions about what kind of planet we want and who we are."[11]

—David Keith, professor of applied physics, Harvard University

WHAT INDIVIDUALS CAN DO

Gail Whiteman, a sustainability expert, and Jeremy Wilkinson, a sea ice physicist, are aware that most people are unfamiliar with Arctic problems such as melting sea ice and melting ice sheets. But they do feel that people can become aware and active by doing three things: paying attention, demanding action, and getting global leaders to convene. Paying attention means keeping up with Arctic changes. For example, the National Snow and Ice Data Center posts daily updates on its web page. The Arctic Sea Ice Forum blog also publishes up-to-date information. Demanding action involves support of companies and politicians who are working toward a low-carbon future. Global leaders must convene and take action, because the Arctic people cannot solve the Arctic's problems by themselves. Climate change is a global problem that requires global action. One key action, according to Wilkinson and Whiteman, is to "keep it in the ground"—that is, not drilling or extracting

TEN WAYS TO STOP GLOBAL WARMING

Individuals can't stop global warming by themselves, but every little bit helps. While nations work to limit fossil fuel use and carbon dioxide emissions, the Natural Resources Defense Council suggests ten ways individuals can help:

» Voice your concerns, especially to elected leaders.

» Power your home with renewable energy.

» Weatherize your home.

» Use energy-efficient appliances.

» Eat less meat, and don't waste food.

» Buy efficient LED lightbulbs.

» Drive a fuel-efficient car.

» Maintain your vehicle to boost efficiency.

» Do less driving and flying.

» Purchase carbon offsets to add clean power to the nation's grid.

existing oil and gas reserves. This will limit emission of greenhouse gases by not removing, transporting, and burning these fossil fuels. It will also help preserve the Arctic, where many of these reserves are located.

Melting Arctic ice is both a regional and a global problem. Slowing or stopping it will require action by the industrialized countries that are most responsible for emitting greenhouse gases. But even if their emission could be stopped today (which it cannot), ice would continue to melt for at least several decades. This means those living in the Arctic will have to adapt to the impacts of rising temperatures in the coming decades. Those in low-lying areas around the world will have to adapt to rising sea levels occurring at least in part from the melting of Arctic ice. Climate change and its impacts will be perhaps the major challenge of the coming decades.

Ongoing changes in the Arctic will affect the lives of people around the world for centuries to come.

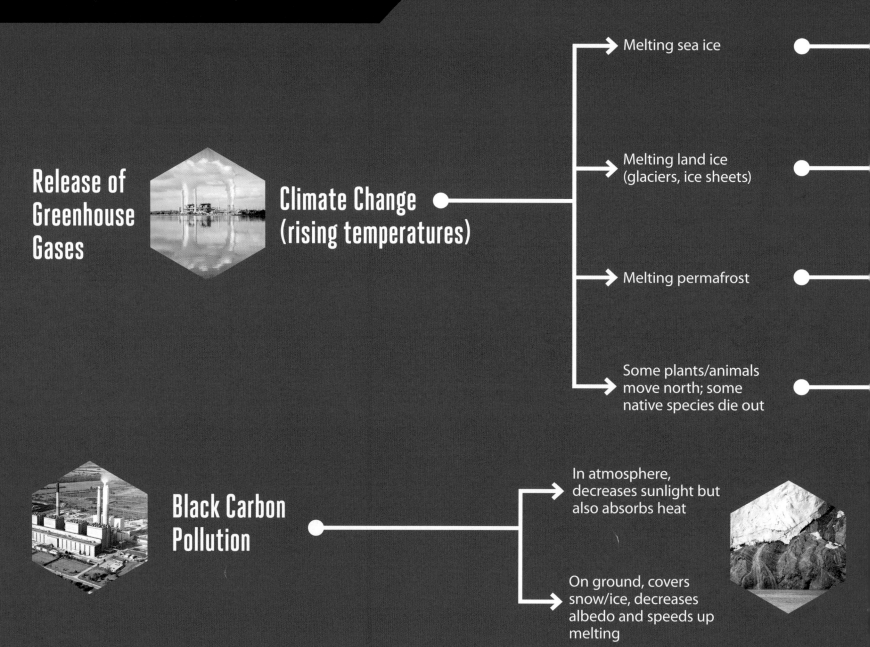

Release of Greenhouse Gases

Climate Change (rising temperatures)

Melting sea ice

Melting land ice (glaciers, ice sheets)

Melting permafrost

Some plants/animals move north; some native species die out

Black Carbon Pollution

In atmosphere, decreases sunlight but also absorbs heat

On ground, covers snow/ice, decreases albedo and speeds up melting

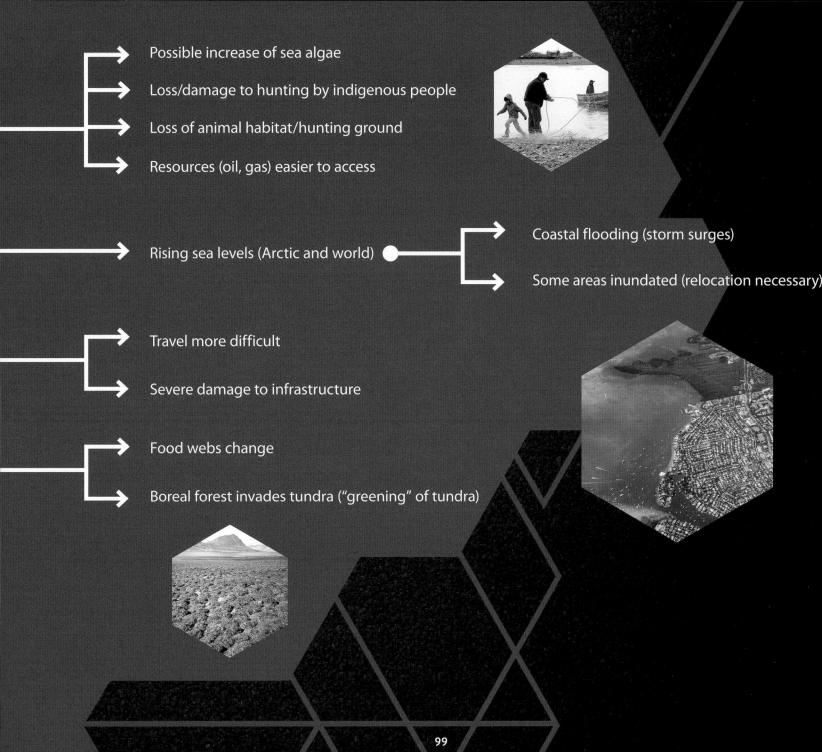

Possible increase of sea algae

Loss/damage to hunting by indigenous people

Loss of animal habitat/hunting ground

Resources (oil, gas) easier to access

Rising sea levels (Arctic and world)

Coastal flooding (storm surges)

Some areas inundated (relocation necessary)

Travel more difficult

Severe damage to infrastructure

Food webs change

Boreal forest invades tundra ("greening" of tundra)

ESSENTIAL FACTS

WHAT IS HAPPENING

The Arctic is undergoing large-scale melting of sea ice, land ice (glaciers and the Greenland ice sheet), and permafrost. This is changing the tundra and endangering the Inuit way of life.

THE CAUSES

The most serious and damaging cause of Arctic ice melt is climate change, which results in higher temperatures. Arctic temperatures are increasing twice as fast as the average global temperature. The high temperatures cause ice to melt more rapidly, uncovering more dark water and soil. The dark areas absorb more (reflect less) heat than white snow and ice; thus, melting sets up a positive feedback loop that amplifies further melting. In addition to climate change, industries in the far north and airplane flights over the North Pole add black carbon (soot) to the atmosphere and ground. In the atmosphere, soot blocks some sunlight but also absorbs heat. On the ground, it produces a black coating that also absorbs heat, increasing melting.

WHEN AND WHERE IT'S HAPPENING

Climate change is a worldwide phenomenon, but its effects are particularly intense in the Arctic. This is the area that surrounds the Arctic Circle (66°34′ north latitude) and encompasses the tundra biome. There is no continent covering the North Pole, only an ocean covered with sea ice, but eight countries, including the United States, have land surrounding the Arctic Ocean. Melting of land and sea ice, as well as permafrost, is occurring throughout the region. Melting occurs in the summers, with partial refreezing during the winters. In the last several decades, melting has overtaken freezing, and most areas are losing ice each year.

KEY PLAYERS

People around the world are contributing to the melting Arctic, because we all contribute to climate change by burning fossil fuels, either directly or indirectly. Many scientists and conservationists are working to understand and slow the processes at work in the Arctic. Along with world leaders, they are also looking for ways to slow the melting, to help people adapt to the changes, and to combat global warming on a global scale. Many Americans working toward these goals work at the National Snow and Ice Data Center in Boulder, Colorado; the National Ocean Service; the National Park Service; and NASA's Goddard Space Flight Center, which uses satellites to monitor changes in the ice.

WHAT IT MEANS FOR THE FUTURE

Impacts in the Arctic are expected to intensify. These include more rapid melting, leading to an ice-free Arctic Ocean during the summer, possibly within a decade. Less ice will make ship transport easier and will increase the likelihood of oil spills resulting from oil and gas exploration and extraction. Less ice will make life more difficult for the Inuit people, who depend on it for hunting, and for animals, such as polar bears and seals, that live most of their lives on the ice. Melting permafrost is already having major impacts on both human infrastructure and natural ecosystems. These will also intensify. Warming temperatures are causing southern plants and animals to migrate north into the Arctic. A major impact, both in the Arctic and in low-lying areas around the world, is sea level rise due to melting Arctic land ice. This will increase the height of storm surges and ultimately cause inundation of many coastal areas and islands.

QUOTE

"Climate change is already happening in the Arctic, faster than its ecosystems can adapt. Looking at the Arctic is like looking at the canary in the coal mine for the entire Earth system."

—Charles Miller, NASA Jet Propulsion Laboratory, 2013

GLOSSARY

basal slip

The process of downhill movement of glaciers by sliding on their base.

cairn

A mound of stones built as a landmark.

calving

The breaking off of a chunk of ice on the edge of a glacier, after which the ice falls into the ocean, forming an iceberg.

carbon sink

A part of the natural environment, such as a forest or ocean, capable of absorbing and storing carbon.

glacier

A large, thickened mass of ice formed from fallen snow that has compacted and been added to over many years.

greenhouse gas

A gas that absorbs infrared radiation and traps heat in the atmosphere.

ice floe

An individual piece of pack ice (sea ice) of 66 feet (20 m) or more in diameter.

ice sheet

The largest category of glacier, consisting of a huge mass of ice on land.

iceberg

A chunk of freshwater ice (made of compacted snow) that breaks off a glacier on land and falls into the sea.

indigenous

Originating in or native to a place.

infrastructure

The physical structures, such as roads, railways, and power plants, that make it possible for a city or nation to function.

pack ice

A general term for sea ice.

peat

Soil formed from partially decomposed plant matter, typically found in cold, boggy, acidic ground.

permafrost

Permanently frozen soil characteristic of the tundra biome.

phytoplankton

Tiny floating algae that form the base of most ocean food webs.

positive feedback loop

A situation in which a process amplifies its own effect upon itself.

sea ice

Ice formed when seawater freezes.

tundra

The biome surrounding the North Pole; the coldest biome on Earth, characterized by permafrost and lack of trees.

zooplankton

Tiny floating animals that feed on phytoplankton.

ADDITIONAL RESOURCES

SELECTED BIBLIOGRAPHY

Environmental Protection Agency. "Climate Change Science: Future of Climate Change." *EPA*. EPA, 29 Sept. 2016. Web. 27 Oct. 2016.

GreenFacts. "Arctic Climate Change." *Digests*. GreenFacts Scientific Board, 29 Sept. 2016. Web. 25 Oct. 2016.

National Snow and Ice Data Center. "Cryosphere: All About the Cryosphere." *NSIDC*. NSIDC, 2016. Web. 6 Nov. 2016.

FURTHER READINGS

Espejo, Roman. *Can Glacier and Icemelt Be Reversed?* Detroit, MI: Greenhaven, 2014. Print.

Lanser, Amanda. *Adapting to Climate Change*. Minneapolis: Abdo, 2015. Print.

Larsen, Eric, and Hudson Lindenberger. *On Thin Ice: An Epic Final Quest into the Melting Arctic*. Guilford, CT: Falcon, 2016. Print.

WEBSITES

To learn more about Ecological Disasters, visit **abdobooklinks.com**. These links are routinely monitored and updated to provide the most current information available.

FOR MORE INFORMATION

For more information on this subject, contact or visit the following organizations:

Goddard Space Flight Center
National Aeronautics and Space Administration (NASA)
8800 Greenbelt Road
Greenbelt, MD 20771
301-286-2000
https://www.nasa.gov/content/water-and-ice

Under its Earth program, the Goddard Space Flight Center studies (among other Earth topics) water, oceans, and ice. Its scientists monitor a fleet of satellites that collects data on oceans and sea ice, and they analyze this data to determine its implications for the present and future.

National Oceanographic and Atmospheric Administration
Arctic Theme Page
1401 Constitution Avenue NW, Room 5128
Washington, DC 20230
301-734-1123
http://www.arctic.noaa.gov

NOAA's Arctic Theme Page is a resource for scientists, students, teachers, decision-makers and the general public—everyone interested in the Arctic. It includes data, graphics, videos, forecasts, and general information of many kinds, including a constantly updated Arctic Report Card.

SOURCE NOTES

CHAPTER 1. HOW DO WE KNOW IT'S MELTING?

1. Geoffrey Mohan. "Message in a Bottle Found 54 Years Later in Arctic." *LA Times*. LA Times, 20 Dec. 2013. Web. 17 Mar. 2017.

2. David Strege. "Message in a Bottle Reveals Fact about Glacier." *GrindTV*. GrindTV, 18 Dec. 2013. Web. 17 Mar. 2017.

3. Ibid.

4. "The Ice Cap." *Greenland*. Greenland.com, n.d. Web. 17 Mar. 2017.

5. "Satellites See Unprecedented Greenland Ice Sheet Surface Melt." *Looking at Earth*. NASA, 24 July 2012. Web. 17 Mar. 2017.

6. Ibid.

7. Julienne Stroeve. "Measuring Fast-Melting Arctic Sea Ice." *Union of Concerned Scientists*. Union of Concerned Scientists, n.d. Web. 17 Mar. 2017.

8. Michael D. Lemonick. "Scientists Turn to Drones for Closer Look at Sea Ice." *Climate Central*. Climate Central, 23 Apr. 2015. Web. 17 Mar. 2017.

9. Julienne Stroeve. "Measuring Fast-Melting Arctic Sea Ice." *Union of Concerned Scientists*. Union of Concerned Scientists, n.d. Web. 17 Mar. 2017.

10. "IceBridge Begins Eighth Year of Arctic Flights." *Earth*. NASA, 20 Apr. 2016. Web. 17 Mar. 2017.

11. "Chasing Ice Movie Reveals Largest Iceberg Break-up Ever Filmed." *Guardian*. Guardian, 12 Dec. 2012. Web. 17 Mar. 2017.

12. Ibid.

13. Amanda Schupak. "Greenland Glacier Loses Chunk the Size of Manhattan." *CBS News*. CBS News, 24 Aug. 2015. Web. 17 Mar. 2017.

14. "Ilulissat Icefjord." *UNESCO*. UN, 2017. Web. 17 Mar. 2017.

15. "Time-Lapse Proof of Extreme Ice Loss." *TED*. TED, Sept. 2009. Web. 17 Mar. 2017.

CHAPTER 2. DEFINING ARCTIC ICE

1. "Tundra Biome." *UCMP*. Berkeley, n.d. Web. 17 Mar. 2017.

2. "Arctic Climate Change." *Green Facts*. Green Facts, 2017. Web. 17 Mar. 2017.

3. "All about Sea Ice." *National Snow and Ice Data Center*. NSIDC, 2017. Web. 17 Mar. 2017.

4. "North Pole an Insane 36 Degrees Warmer Than Normal as Region Hits Record Low Sea Ice Extent." *EcoWatch*. EcoWatch, 18 Nov. 2016. Web. 17 Mar. 2017.

5. "All about Glaciers." *National Snow and Ice Data Center*. NSIDC, 2017. Web. 17 Mar. 2017.

6. Ibid.

7. "Newsroom." *National Snow and Ice Data Center*. NSIDC, 2017. Web. 17 Mar. 2017.

8. "Permafrost in a Warming World." *Weather Underground*. Weather Underground, 2017. Web. 17 Mar. 2017.

9. Joe Romm. "Arctic Death Spiral: Icebreakers Reach North Pole as Sea Ice Disintegrates." *ThinkProgress*. ThinkProgress, 12 Sept. 2016. Web. 17 Mar. 2017.

CHAPTER 3. ARCTIC CLIMATE CHANGE

1. "Temperatures to Rise 0.3-4.8°C This Century, UN Panel Says." *Phys.org*. Phys.org, 27 Sept. 2013. Web. 17 Mar. 2017.

2. "1.5°C vs. 2°C Global Warming: New Study Shows Why Half a Degree Matters." *ScienceDaily*. ScienceDaily, 21 Apr. 2016. Web. 17 Mar. 2017.

3. "Causes of Climate Change." *EPA*. EPA, 27 Dec. 2016. Web. 17 Mar. 2017.

4. Brian Kahn. "The World Passes 400 PPM Threshold. Permanently." *Climate Central*. Climate Central, 27 Sept. 2016. Web. 17 Mar. 2017.

5. "Is a Sleeping Climate Giant Stirring in the Arctic?" *NASA*. NASA, 10 June 2013. Web. 17 Mar. 2017.

6. "Causes of Climate Change." *EPA*. EPA, 27 Dec. 2016. Web. 17 Mar. 2017.

7. "Methane and Black Carbon Impacts on the Arctic." *EPA*. EPA, 2016. Web. 17 Mar. 2017.

8. "Causes of Climate Change." *EPA*. EPA, 27 Dec. 2016. Web. 17 Mar. 2017.

9. "Climate Change Indicators: Snow and Ice." *EPA*. EPA, 2 Aug. 2016. Web. 17 Mar. 2017.

10. "Going, Going…" *Watching the Deniers*. Watching the Deniers, 27 Sept. 2010. Web. 17 Mar. 2017.

11. "Thermodynamics: Albedo." *National Snow and Ice Data Center*. NSIDC, 2017. Web. 17 Mar. 2017.

12. "Andrea Thompson." *Climate Central*. Climate Central, 15 Dec. 2015. Web. 17 Mar. 2017.

13. "2015 Melt Season in Review." *National Snow and Ice Data Center*. NSIDC, 2017. Web. 17 Mar. 2017.

14. "Future of Climate Change." *EPA*. EPA, 27 Dec. 2016. Web. 17 Mar. 2017.

CHAPTER 4. WHAT'S HAPPENING TO ARCTIC ICE?

1. "Arctic Report Card: Update for 2015." *Arctic Program*. NOAA, 15 Dec. 2015. Web. 17 Mar. 2017.

2. Joe Romm. "A Collapse in Arctic Sea Ice Volume Spells Disaster for the Rest of the Planet." *ThinkProgress*. ThinkProgress, 14 Oct. 2016. Web. 17 Mar. 2017.

3. Christopher Joyce. "As July's Record Heat Builds Through August, Arctic Ice Keeps Melting." *The Two-Way*. NPR, 19 Aug. 2016. Web. 17 Mar. 2017.

4. "SOTC: Sea Ice." *National Snow and Ice Data Center*. NSIDC, 1 Nov. 2016. Web. 17 Mar. 2017.

5. "Quick Facts on Ice Sheets." *National Snow and Ice Data Center*. NSIDC, 2017. Web. 17 Mar. 2017.

6. Ibid.

7. "SOTC: Sea Ice." *National Snow and Ice Data Center*. NSIDC, 1 Nov. 2016. Web. 17 Mar. 2017.

8. "Quick Facts on Ice Sheets." *National Snow and Ice Data Center*. NSIDC, 2017. Web. 17 Mar. 2017.

9. Joe Romm. "A Collapse in Arctic Sea Ice Volume Spells Disaster for the Rest of the Planet." *ThinkProgress*. ThinkProgress, 14 Oct. 2016. Web. 17 Mar. 2017.

10. "The Ice Cap." *Greenland*. Greenland.com, n.d. Web. 17 Mar. 2017.

11. "Quick Facts on Ice Sheets." *National Snow and Ice Data Center*. NSIDC, 2017. Web. 17 Mar. 2017.

CHAPTER 5. MELTING ICE AND CHANGING ECOSYSTEMS

1. Lauren Morello. "Thinning Ice Is Turning Arctic into an Algae Hotspot." *Climate Central*. Climate Central, 14 Feb. 2013. Web. 17 Mar. 2017.

2. Doreen Kohlbach, et al. "The Importance of Ice Algae-produced Carbon in the Central Arctic Ocean Ecosystem." *Limnology and Oceanography*. ASLO, Nov. 2016. Web. 17 Mar. 2017.

3. Jon Bowermaster. "Global Warming Changing Inuit Lands, Lives, Arctic Expedition Shows." *National Geographic News*. National Geographic, 15 May 2007. Web. 17 Mar. 2017.

4. Charlie Heck. "Sea Ice Algae Is Staple of Arctic Food Chain." *LiveScience*. LiveScience, 21 Nov. 2014. Web. 17 Mar. 2017.

5. Tia Ghose. "Arctic Temperatures Rising at Breakneck Speed." *LiveScience*. LiveScience, 16 Dec. 2015. Web. 17 Mar. 2017.

6. "Declining Sea Ice Pushes Sea Birds to the Brink." *Conservation*. University of Washington, 6 Jan. 2015. Web. 17 Mar. 2017.

7. "Permafrost." *Wrangell–St. Elias National Park & Preserve, Alaska*. National Park Service, n.d. Web. 17 Mar. 2017.

8. "Declining Sea Ice Pushes Sea Birds to the Brink." *Conservation*. University of Washington, 6 Jan. 2015. Web. 17 Mar. 2017.

9. "Animal Species on Land." *Green Facts*. Green Facts, n.d. Web. 17 Mar. 2017.

10. Michael D. Lemonick. "Thawing Permafrost Will 'Seep, Not Explode' CO2." *Climate Central*. Climate Central, 8 Apr. 2015. Web. 17 Mar. 2017.

11. Bobby Magill. "Arctic Methane Emissions 'Certain to Trigger Warming.'" *Climate Central*. Climate Central, 1 May 2014. Web. 17 Mar. 2017.

12. Michael D. Lemonick. "Thawing Permafrost Will 'Seep, Not Explode' CO2." *Climate Central*. Climate Central, 8 Apr. 2015. Web. 17 Mar. 2017.

13. Ibid.

CHAPTER 6. MELTING ICE AND ARCTIC PEOPLE

1. "Indigenous People: Impacts." *National Snow and Ice Data Center*. NSIDC, 2017. Web. 17 Mar. 2017.

2. Jon Bowermaster. "Global Warming Changing Inuit Lands, Lives, Arctic Expedition Shows." *National Geographic News*. National Geographic, 15 May 2007. Web. 17 Mar. 2017.

3. Ibid.

4. "Publications." *GRID Arendal*. GRID Arendal, n.d. Web. 17 Mar. 2017.

5. Ibid.

6. Ibid.

7. "How Will Infrastructures Be Affected by the Thawing Ground?" *Green Facts*. Green Facts, n.d. Web. 17 Mar. 2017.

8. Jon Bowermaster. "Global Warming Changing Inuit Lands, Lives, Arctic Expedition Shows." *National Geographic News*. National Geographic, 15 May 2007. Web. 17 Mar. 2017.

9. Joaqlin Estus. "Melting Permafrost Threatens Infrastructure, Homes." *Alaska Public Media*. Alaska Public Media, 17 Dec. 2014. Web. 17 Mar. 2017.

CHAPTER 7. MELTING ICE AND RISING SEA LEVELS

1. "North Pole an Insane 36 Degrees Warmer Than Normal as Region Hits Record Low Sea Ice Extent." *EcoWatch*. EcoWatch, 18 Nov. 2016. Web. 17 Mar. 2017.

2. Ibid.

3. "Sea Level Rise." *GlobalChange*. GlobalChange.gov, n.d. Web. 17 Mar. 2017.

4. "Causes of Sea Level Rise: What the Science Tells Us." *Union of Concerned Scientists*. Union of Concerned Scientists, n.d. Web. 17 Mar. 2017.

5. Ibid.

6. Ibid.

7. Ibid.

8. "Is Sea Level Rising?" *National Ocean Service*. NOAA, 22 Dec. 2016. Web. 17 Mar. 2017.

9. "Causes of Sea Level Rise: What the Science Tells Us." *Union of Concerned Scientists*. Union of Concerned Scientists, n.d. Web. 17 Mar. 2017.

10. "New Analysis Shows Global Exposure to Sea Level Rise." *Climate Central*. Climate Central, 23 Sept. 2014. Web. 17 Mar. 2017.

11. "10 Coastal Cities at Greatest Flood Risk as Sea Levels Rise." *Environment News Service*. Environment News Service, 3 Sept. 2013. Web. 17 Mar. 2017.

12. Gwynn Guilford. "An Entire Island Nation Is Preparing to Evacuate to Fiji before They Sink into the Pacific." *Quartz*. Quartz, 1 July 2014. Web. 17 Mar. 2017.

13. Brady Dennis and Chris Mooney. "Scientists Nearly Double Sea Level Rise Projections for 2100, because of Antarctica." *Washington Post*. Washington Post, 30 Mar. 2016. Web. 17 Mar. 2017.

14. Chelsea Harvey. "Melting Arctic Sea Ice Could Be Disrupting the Oceans' Circulation—with Major Consequences." *Washington Post*. Washington Post, 29 June 2015. Web. 17 Mar. 2017.

CHAPTER 8. CAN THE MELTING BE STOPPED?

1. "The Paris Agreement." *United Nations Framework on Climate Change*. United Nations, 2014. Web. 17 Mar. 2017.

2. Eric Osman, Nsikan Akpan, and William Brangham. "Why the Paris Talks Won't Prevent 2 Degrees of Global Warming." *PBS NewsHour*. PBS, 2 Dec. 2015. Web. 17 Mar. 2017.

3. "Future of Climate Change." *EPA*. EPA, 27 Dec. 2016. Web. 17 Mar. 2017.

4. Eric Osman, Nsikan Akpan, and William Brangham. "Why the Paris Talks Won't Prevent 2 Degrees of Global Warming." *PBS NewsHour*. PBS, 2 Dec. 2015. Web. 17 Mar. 2017.

5. Ibid.

6. Ibid.

7. Phil Plait. "Did I Say 30 Billion Tons of CO2 a Year? I Meant 40." *Bad Astronomy Blog*. Slate, 20 Aug. 2014. Web. 17 Mar. 2017.

8. Gail Whiteman and Jeremy Wilkinson. "3 Ways You Can Save the Arctic Ice." *World Economic Forum*. World Economic Forum, 3 Sept. 2015. Web. 17 Mar. 2017.

9. Bob Weber. "One Solution to the Melting Ice Cap: Refreeze It. It Wouldn't Even Cost That Much." *National Post*. National Post, 10 Dec. 2012. Web. 17 Mar. 2017.

10. Paul Salaman. "The Solution for the Melting Polar Ice Caps May Be Hiding in the Rainforest." *Guardian*. Guardian, 11 Jan. 2016. Web. 17 Mar. 2017.

11. Bob Weber. "One Solution to the Melting Ice Cap: Refreeze It. It Wouldn't Even Cost That Much." *National Post*. National Post, 10 Dec. 2012. Web. 17 Mar. 2017.

INDEX

ABOUT THE AUTHOR

Carol Hand has a PhD in zoology with a specialization in marine ecology and a special interest in environmental problems and climate science. Before becoming a science writer, she taught college, wrote for standardized testing companies, and developed multimedia science curricula. She has written approximately 40 books for young people on topics including glaciers and climate change.